BRISTOL MURDERS

Nicola Sly

First published in 2008

Reprinted 2009, 2012

The History Press
The Mill, Brimscombe Port,
Stroud, Gloucestershire, GL5 2QG
www.thehistorypress.co.uk

Copyright © Nicola Sly, 2008

British Library Cataloguing in Publication Data
A catalogue record for this book is available from the
British Library.

ISBN 978-0-7509-5048-0

Typesetting and origination by
The History Press Limited.
Printed and bound in England.

CONTENTS

FOREWORD

For hundreds of years, Bristol has been a seaport of great importance, a bustling, cosmopolitan city renowned for the manufacture of glass, soap, chemicals and earthenware. Yet, as with every great city, behind its prosperous façade are its people and wherever there are large numbers of people, there are inevitably a few 'bad apples' for whom human life holds little or no importance.

In co-writing *Somerset Murders* with John Van der Kiste, I found myself continuously pleading for Bristol to be included, since I had found yet another 'interesting case'. It soon became obvious that Bristol was deserving of its own book, as this collection of accounts of murders within the city between 1741 and 1957 will hopefully demonstrate.

Some of the murders featured were not widely reported outside Bristol, while others shocked the nation. In 1923, George Cooper happily allowed his wife and child to use the sitting room of his home in Brislington for several weeks, knowing that he had concealed the body of his father beneath the floorboards. In 1942, the entire country was horrified by the apparent 'sexual perversions' of Cecil Cornock, found dead in his bath in suspicious circumstances, while the deaths of a young brother and sister, Royston and June Sheasby in 1957, were mourned nationwide.

The collection of cases includes arguments between husbands and wives with tragic consequences, child murders, killings for financial gain, robberies with extreme violence and murders committed by jealous lovers. A handful of cases remain unsolved to this day and there are a few where the apparent killer was subsequently tried and found not guilty – did they literally get away with murder?

There are numerous people who must be acknowledged and thanked for their assistance in compiling this collection. Colin Wilson, John J. Eddleston and the late Veronica Smith have all previously published books either on murder in Bristol or more general reference works on British murders and executions. The memoirs of J.D. Casswell QC, who defended some of the accused, provided a fascinating insight into the complexities of the laws relating to murder. These books are recorded in more detail in the bibliography, as are the local and national newspapers and magazines, which proved an invaluable source of material. My thanks must also go to the staff of Bristol Central Library, both for their help in my research and for permission to use some of the photographs that they hold in their collection.

John Van der Kiste was, as always, a true friend, generously offering assistance and advice. My sister-in-law, Anne Wibberley, helped with research and provided local knowledge, as did Julie Cross. The volunteers at Arnos Vale Cemetery were most helpful, as were John Jones of J & M Classic Cars in Bangor, Gwynedd,

Bristol city centre, 1950s. (Author's collection)

who kindly supplied photographs of his stunning Austin 16 car, and Derek Fisher of Bygone Bristol, who sourced and supplied some of the illustrations.

I must also thank my long-suffering husband, Richard, without whose help and encouragement I would not have been able to write this book. His services as a chauffeur, occasional photographer, proofreader and general critic were invaluable, as was his tolerance of numerous missed meals and a rather untidy home while I was immersed in Bristol's darkest side. His support – and that of my father, John Higginson – were very much appreciated.

Finally, my thanks must go to my editor at Sutton Publishing, Matilda Pearce, for her continued help and encouragement.

1

'LOVE AND FRIENDSHIP'

Off Avonmouth, 1741

Sir John Edward Dineley was a very wealthy man and, after the death of his oldest grandson in a duel, he appointed another grandson, John Goodere, as his heir.

John Goodere was described as a rough and uncouth man of very little education who, having been brought up among merchant seamen, elected to go to sea himself. His younger brother, Samuel, eventually followed him, joining His Majesty's navy in 1705.

John quit his life at sea at his grandfather's insistence to prepare for his inheritance. When his mother died, as the eldest son, he inherited her estate in Worcestershire and John also married well, his wife bringing a mansion at Stapleton to the marriage along with a country mansion at Tockington in South Gloucestershire.

When Sir John Edward Dineley finally died, Samuel was aggrieved that so little of his grandfather's estate came to him. In view of his older brother's independent wealth, Samuel felt that he had not received a large enough legacy and his anger was further fuelled when John – now Sir John – stated that he intended to leave his fortune to two distant cousins rather than to his younger brother.

The bad feeling simmered between the two brothers until 1741, when Samuel determined to murder his brother. By now the captain of HMS *Ruby*, Samuel managed to wangle an invitation to a dinner being given in his brother's honour at a house in College Green. He gathered together a group of men, with the intention of abducting his brother but, in the event, his plans were thwarted when John turned up at the dinner in the company of a well-armed servant. Refusing to see his brother, John conducted some business with Bristol solicitor Jarritt Smith, then went home.

Samuel set up another appointment for 20 January 1741 and again readied his band of sixteen sailors and ruffians, stowing them in the nearby White Hart Inn. This time, the meeting between the two brothers at the home of Jarritt Smith

College Green: scene of the last meeting between John Goodere and his murderer. (Author's collection)

was more convivial. They greeted each other with a kiss, enjoyed an amicable conversation and ended their meeting with a toast to 'love and friendship'. After parting, Samuel met up with his gang from the pub, while Sir John walked alone to the quayside.

It was there that Matthew Mahoney, the leader of Samuel's band of men, jumped him, the gang then bundling Sir John onto the barge of HMS *Ruby*, which was moored at the Mardyke. Telling startled onlookers that their prisoner was a murderer who was about to face trial aboard ship, the captive was taken on board the *Ruby* where Samuel had him placed below decks, telling his shipmates that he was insane and had to be locked up and guarded. Sometime between 2 a.m. and 3 a.m., crewman Charles White, who was extremely drunk at the time, crept into the cabin with the intention of silencing Sir John's shouts and preventing him from awakening the whole ship. White stuffed a handkerchief into the prisoner's mouth and then strangled him with a piece of rope. With his last breath, Sir John was heard to gasp, 'Oh my poor life.'

With Sir John finally silenced, Samuel locked the cabin door and took Mahoney and White back to his own cabin. There Mahoney handed over Sir John's gold watch and, in return, was given Samuel's silver one. Mahoney and White each received a payment of around £14 for their work, with White receiving a slightly larger amount of money since Mahoney had received the watch.

It is not known how Samuel intended to dispose of his brother's body but his plans became irrelevant due to the actions of the ship's cooper. Claiming to have witnessed the murder through a chink in the cabin wall, the cooper informed the ship's carpenter of what he had seen and the carpenter immediately broke down the cabin door, revealing the corpse.

Even with a dead body in plain view, the ship's officers were reluctant to take action, so the cooper, backed up by ten other crewmembers, took it upon himself to arrest Captain Goodere.

Mahoney and White were later apprehended in a Bristol alehouse. Each made voluntary confessions to their part in the murder, both laying the blame for the actual killing on the other. Samuel – now Sir Samuel since the death of his brother – was more brazen. He continued to allege that his brother was insane and denied any part in his murder, asking why, as heir to the family estate, he would risk losing an inheritance of £40,000 by killing his brother.

He was sent to Bristol's Newgate Gaol where authorities installed a new iron plated cell door, fearful that his gang might try to spring him from prison. Finally, with the death penalty awaiting him, Sir Samuel confessed his guilt, while Mahoney and White both stated that they had been almost insensible with drink at the time of the murder. Goodere appealed to the Crown for mercy, as did his wife and daughter on his behalf, but their appeals were rejected and, on 15 April 1741, all three conspirators were executed.

Captain Goodere's body was taken for dissection, while Mahoney's body was hung on a gibbet pole on Dunball, an island just off Avonmouth, close to the place where the *Ruby* had been moored when the murder was committed. The gibbet pole on the island was intended to serve as a warning to lawless seamen sailing into the Bristol Docks and it survived as a grim reminder to would-be wrongdoers until the middle of the nineteenth century.

[Note: As might be expected, there is some variation in dates in contemporary accounts of this murder. The date of the actual killing is variously given as 19 and 20 January 1741 and the date of the execution of the perpetrators as 15 and 17 April.]

2

'OH LORD, I AM KILLED'

Hanham, 1821

John Horwood was born in April 1803, the last of the ten children of Thomas Horwood, an ex-seaman. Like most boys in the area at the time, John was set to work in the coal mining industry as soon as he was old enough, but the pits had proved rather tragic for the Horwood family. One of John's brothers, Joseph, was seriously injured in a mining accident at the age of 15 and Joseph's twin brother, James, was killed when the roof of the mine in which he was working caved in.

John was never very happy working in the mines and, after two years, he was delighted to be offered a position in Philip George's Spelter Works in Hanham. He was an industrious boy and a regular attendee at chapel – or at least, he was until around the time of his sixteenth birthday. The cause off his sudden change in character was a young girl, Eliza Balsum, who was some eighteen months his senior.

John, a small, rather stout youth, fancied himself in love with Eliza and his feelings for her were so strong that he soon abandoned his job in order to spend more time in her company. He deceived his parents, persuading them to buy clothes for him so that he could look smart while supposedly seeking work, and turned to a life of petty crime as a source of cash. On one occasion, he and Eliza's brother were arrested together and served a short sentence in prison.

It is not known whether the attraction between John and Eliza was at first mutual, but by 1820, John was making Eliza's life a misery by what we today would call stalking. He was relentless in his pursuit of the poor girl, making indecent suggestions to her, threatening her life and vowing to burn her parents' house down. Once, he even threw vitriol over her, the acid burning holes through her clothes but fortunately failing to cause Eliza any serious injury.

The motive for Horwood's obsessive behaviour was undoubtedly a combination of unrequited love and jealousy. He vowed to be the death of Eliza should he ever catch her with another man.

Hanham Mills, 2007. (©N. Sly)

Eliza became very nervous of leaving home after the acid attack, but on Christmas night she was outside and spotted John hanging about near her house. Her mother heard her banging frantically on the door to be let in and, once the door was opened, Eliza rushed inside in a panic, telling her mother that John had said he was going to 'burn her all to pieces'. Her mother, Sarah, opened the window and confronted John, who was still lurking just outside the house. She asked him why he was threatening her child and Horwood replied that he would kill Eliza and all those who took her part. Sarah threatened him with a warrant, to which he responded, 'You may fetch a warrant and be damned!'

The Balsums' next-door neighbour, Samuel Rogers, witnessed the incident but was too frightened to intervene; fearing that the angry youth would 'knock his brains out'. The Balsum family eventually chased Horwood off, but, as he fled, he shouted back a threat that he would mash Eliza's bones as small as ashes when he finally caught her.

On 30 or 31 January 1821, John was out walking with three friends, brothers Joseph and Samuel Fry and Thomas Barnes. Although it was after eight o'clock at night and dark at the time, Horwood spotted Eliza by the light of the moon. She too was out with friends, namely two local young men, Joseph Reece and William Waddy.

As the two groups approached each other, Horwood picked up a large stone, which he threw at Eliza as hard as he could. The stone hit her on the right-hand side of her head, causing her to topple into a small brook, pulling Waddy in after her. As she fell, she cried out, 'Oh Lord, I am killed.'

Her two companions carried her home, where her horrified mother put her to bed. Eliza had a black eye, severe bruising and a large cut on the right-hand side her forehead, which Sarah dressed with a bread and milk poultice. Over the next few days, Eliza suffered from vomiting attacks and complained of being in great pain and, when there was no improvement in her condition after five days, she was taken to Bristol Infirmary. An unrepentant John Horwood was heard to say that if Eliza didn't die there, then he would be damned if he didn't kill her when she came out.

Shortly after her admission to hospital, the sheriff's yeomen arrived at the door of Horwood's parents' cottage to arrest the young man. Having first tried to escape through his bedroom window, but finding it too small, Horwood determined to go down fighting, charging at yeomen officers Bull and Sew, swinging a hammer.

Officer Bull was slightly injured as Horwood flung the hammer at him in desperation, but the combined strength of the two men soon overpowered the youth and he was frogmarched to Eliza Balsum's bedside to hear her deposition. In her statement, Eliza related how Horwood had persistently made indelicate and improper proposals to her and that she had 'constantly refused to yield to his solicitations.' As a consequence, Horwood had waylaid her several times, always threatening to kill her. She could remember very little about the stone-throwing incident, save that she had actually seen Horwood throwing the stone. When it hit her head, she fell down and could recall nothing more. When Horwood was asked if he wanted to ask her any questions, he simply said no. Meanwhile, Eliza lay trembling in her hospital bed, too frightened even to look at him.

Eliza lost her fight to live on 17 February, the cause of her death being determined as a depressed fracture of her skull. Horwood was promptly charged with her murder. He stood trial at the Lent Assizes in Bristol, the proceedings opening on 11 April 1821.

The court heard from two of the friends who had accompanied Horwood on the night of the attack on Eliza Balsum. Samuel Fry recalled that he had not seen Eliza, but had heard a woman cry out. His companion, Thomas Barnes, had immediately commented that, 'It was a shame', but Fry maintained that he hadn't known to what Barnes was referring.

Barnes described standing with his companions at the four-crossroads in Hanham, between 35yds and 40yds from the brook. He had seen Horwood raise his arm and make a throwing motion, but had not noticed anything in his hand. Immediately afterwards, he had heard a splash and the sound of a woman's voice crying out, although he had only been able to distinguish the words 'Oh, Lord'. Barnes had commented that there was 'someone knocked down in the bottom', but stated that he was unable to see anything. Ten minutes later, Horwood had told Barnes not to talk about the incident, but Barnes was unable to keep the secret.

About a week later, he had met Horwood by chance and had been called 'a deluding son of a *****' for discussing what he had seen. Later still, Horwood had threatened to fight him, although Barnes insisted that they had parted on good terms.

Other witnesses tried unsuccessfully to provide John Horwood with an alibi for the time of the attack on Eliza Balsum.

Sarah Balsum told the court about the incident on Christmas night, when Horwood had followed Eliza home, and her neighbour, Samuel Rogers, corroborated her account. She also related Eliza's condition after the stone throwing incident, and told how she had tried to nurse Eliza at home before her admission to hospital.

The senior surgeon at the Bristol Infirmary spoke of Eliza's treatment, death and the post-mortem examination, at which it was discovered that the stone had fractured her skull, causing her death. Then Eliza's deposition was read to the court.

Next, counsels for the defence and the prosecution summed up their cases for the jury, at which point John Horwood was asked if he had anything to say in his defence. 'I leave my defence to my counsellor' was his surly reply.

The judge then spoke to the jury, telling them that, in the eyes of the law, if a person threw a stone with the intent of only afflicting a 'partial mischief' and death ensued, then the crime would be murder.

The jury retired, returning after one hour and forty minutes with a verdict of 'Guilty of Wilful Murder' against the defendant. It was not without emotion that the judge reached for his black cap and his voice faltered and trembled as he pronounced the death sentence on 17-year-old Horwood. The judge was not the only person to show emotion – Horwood had sat unmoved throughout the entire proceedings, but when he heard his fate, a few tears were seen to trickle down his cheeks and he dabbed at them with his handkerchief.

Horwood was taken to Bristol New Gaol on Cumberland Road to await his execution. His was to be the first held at the New Gaol, and the prison carpenter, Mr Wilmot, had already prepared well for the event, having visited Gloucester Prison to examine the 'drop' located there. Wilmot eventually built a replica of the Gloucester execution platform, at a cost of £30.

Confined in prison, John Horwood reverted to his strict chapel upbringing, making a full confession to the murder of Eliza, saying, 'Lord, thou knowest that I did not mean then to take away her life but merely to punish her: though I confess that I made up my mind, some time or other, to murder her.'

The gatehouse on Cumberland Road is all that remains of the Bristol New Gaol. (©R. Sly)

On the morning of Friday 13 April, just three days after his eighteenth birthday, Horwood was escorted to the gallows. A crowd of 40,000 people had assembled outside the prison to watch the spectacle but Horwood made them all wait. It was the privilege of the person being executed to hold a handkerchief in their hand, which they dropped as a signal to the executioner that they were ready to die. Horwood clutched the handkerchief tightly in his hand for no less than twenty-five minutes before he found the courage to let it fall. When the handkerchief finally dropped, his death came very quickly.

Friends and relatives of Horwood had hoped to thwart plans to hand his body over to surgeon Richard Smith, to be used in his dissection classes for student doctors at the Bristol Royal Infirmary. They lay in wait outside the prison planning to ambush the cart bearing his body, and then return Horwood's remains by boat to Hanham. However, the authorities had anticipated such an occurrence and sent the body to the hospital under the cover of night.

Having used the corpse of John Horwood to teach his students the principles of anatomy, Smith had the skin preserved and tanned and commissioned a bookbinder to use it to bind a large ledger detailing the murder, trial and execution. The skin-covered book was embossed with a skull and crossbones at each corner and the front cover was gilded with the words, *Cutis Vera Johannis Horwood* – 'The Skin of John Horwood'. The bookbinder's bill for £10 is still tucked inside it to this day.

The book is now safely kept at the Bristol Record Office. Over the years, it has become too fragile to allow the public direct access to it, but its contents have been faithfully recorded on microfiche.

The gruesome book was not the only legacy that Horwood left behind. While imprisoned and confined in his cell awaiting his execution, he penned a short poem, which was later printed out and sold to the crowds on the day of his execution. The poem reads:

John Horwood is my wretched name
And Hanham gave me birth
My previous time has been employed
In rioting and mirth.

Eliza, Oh Eliza Dear!
Thy spirit, Oh, is fled!
And thy poor mangled body lies
Now number'd with the dead.

Curs'd is the hand that gave the blow
And Curs'd the fatal stone
Which made thy precious life blood flow
For it has me undone.

3

'MIND, MARY. YOU KNOW NOTHING ABOUT IT'

St Philips, 1833

Mary Ann Williams was a fresh-faced country girl from Orcop, near Ross-on-Wye in Herefordshire. She came to Bristol seeking work and was engaged as a house servant by Mr Plumley, a poulterer from Nicholas Street. However, after eighteen months, Plumley could take no more of Mary Ann's thieving ways and dismissed her. Not only was she sacked, but Plumley also refused to give her a reference.

An indignant Mary Ann immediately consulted a solicitor and gave him instructions to sue Plumley for £50, but by the time the case was due to come to court at the Taunton Assizes, Mary Ann had married a tailor named Mr Agar and had lost interest in claiming damages against her former employer.

Mary Ann obviously found married life with the respectable tailor too tame as she soon deserted him to run away with a married coachman, Mr Thomas. Then, when a better prospect came along in the form of a wealthy Bristol merchant, Mary Ann had no qualms about leaving the coachman and moving on.

With her newfound prosperity, Mary Ann saved enough money to rent a house in Limekiln Lane, which she promptly turned into a brothel. Her neighbours were far from happy about the constant procession of sailors arriving at the house and eventually she was hounded from the street.

Her next beau was Mr Wade, a steward on one of the Bristol steam packets who also owned a clothing shop. Having met in a pub, Wade and Mary Ann decided to join forces, operating a lodging house at 17 Trinity Street, St Philips. Before long, Wade died and Mary Ann subsequently married one of the lodgers, a Mr Burdock.

Into the lodging house came Mrs Clara Ann Smith, a sickly woman with a permanent hacking cough. Knowing that Clara Smith was the widow of an

9

ironmonger from Old Market Street, who had left his widow a fortune of £3,000 on his death, Mary Ann made it her business to get close to the frail elderly lady, neglecting her other boarders to care personally for Mrs Smith. It seemed that nothing was too much trouble for the devoted nurse and, before long, Mary Ann had persuaded Clara to hand over her life savings for safekeeping. Mary Ann used some of the money to pay off her own debts – mostly for the purchase of clothes – and banked the remaining £500. It was then obviously in Mary Ann's interests to hasten the death of Mrs Smith and accordingly, she sent her husband out to buy two pennyworth of arsenic, which she fed to Mrs Smith in a bowl of warm gruel.

The elderly woman died on or about 26 August 1833 and was hastily buried in the graveyard of St Augustine's Church, with Mr and Mrs Burdock her only mourners. Her relatives – a nephew and three nieces – were not even informed of her death. When they eventually found out fourteen months later, they began to wonder what had happened to her considerable fortune and quickly took their concerns to the police.

Even though the death of Mrs Smith was now the subject of a police investigation, Mary Ann was not at all concerned, no doubt feeling that she had successfully covered her tracks. After all, her victim was safely buried and she had destroyed every scrap of paperwork relating to Mrs Smith's finances. However, she had reckoned without Mary Ann Allen, a young servant girl who worked in the lodging house at the time of the victim's death.

Mary Ann Allen told police that she had seen her mistress pouring some yellow powder into a bowl of milky gruel, which she then gave to Mrs Smith.

Bristol Guildhall and Halls of Justice. (Author's collection)

As a result of Mary Ann Allen's statement, police arranged for Mrs Smith to be exhumed. In the dead of night, her body was removed from the grave and examined by a team of doctors and surgeons from the Bristol Infirmary.

Arsenic acts as a preservative when ingested and the doctors found that Mrs Smith's body was so well preserved that it was later used as an example in medical textbooks. The police now felt that they had a cast-iron case against Mary Ann Burdock and she was arrested and committed for trial at the Guildhall.

Rather indignantly, Mary Ann Burdock pleaded not guilty to the wilful murder of Clara Smith. She described Smith as a dirty old woman who constantly spat phlegm and blood all over her clothes and pointed out that her lodger was behind with the rent. Mary Ann insisted that she had treated the elderly woman with nothing but kindness, fetching titbits of food such as custard puddings to try and tempt her to eat and providing brandy, rum and wine. She added that she had tried to persuade Mrs Smith to consult a doctor about her failing health but Mrs Smith had refused, saying that she did not want a doctor to murder her.

The prosecution called numerous witnesses, all of whom testified to Clara Smith's cleanliness and to the extent of her personal fortune. Then PC Griffiths, who had been sent to Mrs Burdock's to ask another servant, Mary Evans, for an interview, related that Burdock had repeatedly told the girl, 'Mind, Mary. You know nothing about it.'

With the weight of evidence against her, the outcome of Mary Ann Burdock's three-day trial seemed to be a foregone conclusion and at the end, the judge passed the only possible sentence. Having first assured the prisoner that she had received a fair trial and that the laborious investigation into her crime had established her guilt so conclusively that no jury could possibly have found her innocent, he then ordered that she be taken to a place of execution and hanged by the neck until dead.

Although she apparently experienced a fainting fit on arrival at the prison, once confined in Bristol New Gaol awaiting her execution, Mary Ann Burdock remained in firm control of her emotions, seemingly indifferent to her fate. Having rebuked her defence counsel for what she considered the mismanagement of her trial, she turned her attention to the money she had obtained from her victim, which was still in the bank. Asking what would remain after all the bills had been paid, she expressed a wish that, after her death, the money should go to her two children, a boy aged 15 and a girl of 8 or 9. Although Mary Ann seemed to derive great comfort at the thought of her children inheriting the money, in reality it was unlikely that they would benefit, particularly since Clara Smith's relatives had already made a claim. It was thought that the Bristol Corporation might also be entitled to recover some of the money, having born the cost of staging both the trial and execution.

Next, Mary Ann Burdock summoned the matron of the gaol to enquire who made the prison coffins and proceeded to give her brother, who was visiting her at the time, precise instructions on how she would like her own coffin made. She insisted that it must be a full-sized coffin, lined with flannel, with a comfortable shroud to keep her warm – she also stressed that her brother should not pay more than £2. The elm coffin was fashioned exactly to her specifications and brought to her cell for inspection on the eve of her execution. Having examined the coffin

Mary Ann Burdock. (By kind permission of Bristol Central Library)

closely, Mary Ann grudgingly conceded that it would do. She slept soundly that night, the coffin remaining by her bed.

She spent the last hours before her execution in the prison chapel with other prisoners, one of whom was her husband who had been imprisoned for debt. Sitting silently in the pew, neither rising nor kneeling during the solemn service performed by the Revd Mr Jennings, the only emotion she portrayed was a slight sigh when the commandment 'Thou shalt do no murder' was intoned.

Various accounts of the execution in contemporary newspapers differ in opinion as to whether or not Mary Ann confessed to the murder. One states that, even in the face of heartfelt pleas from her son, Mary Ann continued to insist that she would die an innocent woman. Others say that she 'manifested the deepest penitence for her offences', while another details her full confession, apparently made to the prison matron. Regardless of whether or not she had actually repented her sins, Mary Ann Burdock – allegedly one of the first poisoners ever to use arsenic – had an appointment with the hangman on Wednesday 15 April 1835.

Dressed in a black gown and bonnet with a coloured shawl, she was escorted by the prison governor to the press room, where her bonnet and shawl were removed and the rope placed around her neck, at which she asked if something soft could be put around it. She seemed to want to linger in the press room and, when urged to proceed, replied with the words, 'Dear gentlemen, the time is short – it is hard to die.' As she progressed towards the gallows, she asked to be remembered to her husband and friends.

A crowd of almost 50,000 people assembled outside the prison to watch the execution and, as the figures of Mary Ann Burdock and the executioner appeared at the scaffold, the crowd suddenly stopped jostling for the best view and fell silent. Mary Ann, who wore a white hood over her face, dropped the handkerchief she had been clutching in her trembling hand as a signal to the executioner, who quickly drew the bolt. Her body was buried within the confines of the prison grounds, marked by a headstone, which was inscribed:

Beneath this stone lie the remains of
MARY ANN BURDOCK
who was executed in this Gaol, April 15 1835,
in her 38th year,
for the wilful murder (by Poison) of
Clara Ann Smith,
of this City

[Note: Mary Ann Burdock's age at the time of her execution is variously given as 30 years, 34 years and 38 years.]

13

4

'I HAVE NOTHING TO SAY'

Redland, 1839

In 1839, the Redland area of Bristol was a green and pleasant rural place, dotted with farms. One of these was Coldharbour, a dairy farm owned by Mr Richard Warre. Warre employed several young farmhands, all of whom shared accommodation in the farmhouse. Until recently, William Davis had been one of these employees but he had been dismissed for 'improper conduct'.

In the early afternoon of Saturday 9 February, another farmhand, 19-year-old John Butt, was working in the barn in a field adjoining Coldharbour Lane. He was interrupted by William Davis, who casually remarked on the good quality of the hay with which he was feeding the cows. Davis and Butt had lived and worked together without quarrel until Davis left the farm under a cloud. Now, Davis asked Butt how long he was going to be and Butt replied that he would only be staying for as long as it took to finish the feeding. With that, Davis turned on his heel and left abruptly.

Having finished his chores, Butt was walking back along Redland Lane when he again saw Davis standing in the roadway, peering over a hedge. Butt bade him 'Good afternoon' and continued walking. However, no sooner had he passed Davis than he felt a blow on the back of his head, which knocked him to the ground. As he tried to get to his feet, he felt another blow, which rendered him unconscious.

When Butt came round, he found himself lying on the lane in a pool of blood. His pockets had been turned out and his watch and money stolen. Butt managed to crawl about 30yds towards the end of the lane, where Samuel Roberts, a milkman, heard his cries for help. By the time Roberts located the source of the cries, John Butt had collapsed again. He lay face down at the side of the road, his clothes drenched with blood.

Roberts was unable to lift Butt, so he ran to a nearby house for assistance, returning with a cart driven by Mr Lowless, a tanner. Together, the two men tried to help Butt to his feet but he was incapable of standing so they lifted him onto the cart and drove him to Durdham Downs, from where he was conveyed to Bristol Royal Infirmary.

There, surgeon Richard Smith found eight wounds on Butt's head, which, in his opinion, must have been caused by eight separate blows. One of the blows had

14

been sufficiently violent to fracture Butt's skull. Smith and other doctors agreed that the most appropriate treatment at that stage was trepanning – the removal of a section of the skull to reduce pressure on the brain – and this was done. In view of the seriousness of Butt's injuries, magistrates were called to his bedside to take his deposition, in which he identified Davis as his assailant.

Davis was known to the Bristol police, who were aware that he had connections in Chepstow. Consequently, on 10 February, PC John White was sent to the Old Passage at Aust, about twelve miles from Bristol, from where there was a regular ferry service to Chepstow. Dressed in plain clothes, White was leaning on a wall at the passage house when he saw Davis arrive. He promptly arrested and searched him, finding several of the items that had been reported stolen by Butt. These included money and, most damning, a fourpenny piece with a hole drilled through it.

White escorted Davis to the police station at Bristol, then at 6 p.m. that evening, he was taken to the infirmary. In the presence of Davis and two magistrates, the fourpenny piece was shown to John Butt, who identified it as the one he normally wore on his watch chain.

PC Henry Phillips-Webb was sent to search Davis's lodgings and a pawn ticket bearing the name George Smith was found in his room. This proved to be from a pawnshop in Bristol and when the shop was visited, attendant Barbara Salmon produced a silver watch, engraved with the name J. Butt, against which she had advanced 1*s* to a man calling himself George Smith. Salmon identified Davis as being the 'George Smith' who had pawned the watch.

Davis was detained in Bristol Gaol. As was customary at the time, to prevent prisoners from committing suicide, he shared a cell with two other prisoners, Charles Burdon and John Kennedy. Seeing that Davis seemed ill at ease, Burdon asked him what the matter was, at which Davis broke down and confessed to his two cellmates that he had hit Butt over the head with a stick, which he described as having a large knob as big as his fist on the end.

John Butt died from his wounds four days after being admitted to hospital and, according to the doctors treating him, was fully aware of his circumstances until about twelve hours before his death. At his post-mortem examination, it was revealed that most of the blows to Butt's head had penetrated his skull and were without doubt the cause of his death. William Davis was immediately charged with his wilful murder.

Davis's case was heard before Mr Justice Erskine at Gloucester Crown Court. The trial opened at the beginning of April 1839, with Mr Watson and Mr Skinner acting for the prosecution and Mr MacLean defending.

It was an open and shut case. The jury listened to Butt's deposition and heard evidence from the surgeons at Bristol Hospital. The two prisoners, Burdon and Kennedy, testified to Davis's confession and the pawn shop assistant, Barbara Salmon, linked Davis to Butt's watch, which had been stolen in the course of the vicious attack. The police officers strengthened this link by showing that, when arrested, Davis was in possession of several more items stolen from the victim, including the unique fourpenny piece.

The jury were quick to find Davis guilty and the death sentence was passed, to which Davis simply responded, 'I have nothing to say.' He was hanged at Gloucester Prison on 20 April 1839, aged 22 years.

5

'GOOD GOD! HERE IS YOUR MOTHER ON THE FLOOR'

Horfield, 1841

In 1841, Horfield was largely populated by retired tradesmen from the city of Bristol. One of its inhabitants was Mr Alexander Shedden, a retired apothecary, who had recently moved to Horfield from Kingsdown with his wife, Martha.

Mr Shedden owned several properties in the area and, on 20 January, he announced his intention of going into Bristol to collect some rent. Telling Martha that he didn't expect to be home for dinner, he set off at about 10.30 a.m., leaving his 67-year-old wife to look after her 96-year-old bedridden mother and to prepare for the arrival of some expected guests.

Shortly after leaving the house, Shedden met a young man who had previously done some gardening work for him and had also helped to move furniture when the Sheddens had taken possession of their new home during the previous September. After exchanging greetings, Shedden asked 16-year-old Charles Rudge where he was going and was told that he was heading to Horfield to do some work at the Academy.

Having concluded his business in the city, Shedden took tea with his son, Henry, then set off to walk home, accompanied by Henry and Henry's son. The three stopped briefly at the Wagon and Horses public house at 7.15 p.m., where they each drank a glass of beer.

Arriving at the Sheddens' home about fifteen minutes later, they were surprised to see it in complete darkness. Shedden tapped on the front door with his walking stick but received no response. Thinking that his wife may have gone to visit a neighbour, he set off to find out, but was quickly called back by Henry who had thought to try the back door and found it unlocked.

The kitchen was dark and the fire was out. Shedden knew that a box of matches was usually kept on the mantelpiece, but as he inched his way across the dark room to find them, he stumbled over something that felt very much like a body. 'Good God!' he exclaimed to his son, 'Here is your mother on the floor – she must have fallen in a fit.' When he struck a match and lit a lamp, it was to discover that his wife was not ill, but dead. Martha Shedden lay on her left side, her skirts pulled up around her knees as if someone had been rifling through her pockets. The floor was awash with blood, which had also spattered liberally over the walls of the kitchen.

A surgeon, Mr J.H. Bell, was immediately sent for. When he arrived at 8.30 p.m., his first thoughts were that Mrs Shedden had been shot and it was only on closer examination that he noted the many severe wounds on her head and face. Over her right ear were three cuts, two superficial and one exposing brain matter beneath it. Another wound with a corresponding skull fracture was found above her left ear, with a further injury to the crown of the back of her head. She also had several large cuts on her face.

Bell noted that the wounds on the left-hand side were incised and those on the right were contused. He believed that the same weapon had caused all the injuries and suggested it was probably a large hammer, with one striking and one cutting edge, such as those used by plasterers when lathing. Mrs Shedden's hair was down and the hairpiece that she normally wore had fallen into the pool of blood near the kitchen chair.

It was Bell's opinion that Mrs Shedden would have been stunned by the first blows but might well have survived for some five or ten minutes after the initial attack. From the position of her arms, he felt that she might have grappled with her attacker.

Suspicion immediately fell on Charles Rudge who, it seemed, had not only argued with the Sheddens in the past but had also been seen by neighbours helping Mrs Shedden to beat carpets on the day of her murder. Thus police went straight to his father's house at Alfred Court, Kingsdown, arriving at about midnight. Rudge's mother answered the door and anxiously led the officers upstairs to where her son was asleep in bed. When woken by the police and told that an old woman had been murdered at Horfield, Rudge allegedly mentioned Mrs Shedden's name before any of the arresting officers had identified the victim to him.

Rudge dressed, apparently in the clothes he had been wearing earlier that day, which lay on his bed. Tearfully protesting his innocence, he was taken to Lawford's Gate Prison where he was detained by magistrates pending the outcome of the coroner's inquest.

The inquest was held before coroner Mr William Joyner Ellis, opening on 27 January. The jury, in the company of the accused, were first taken to view the body of Mrs Shedden, with Rudge again protesting his innocence of her murder. The inquest then heard testimony from Alexander Shedden.

Having recounted his trip to Bristol on the day of the murder and the gruesome discovery that awaited him on his return, Shedden stated that the house appeared to have been searched. Drawers were found open, one of which had been forced and some loose silver coinage kept in a tin box had been stolen. According to Shedden, Rudge was well aware that money was kept in the box.

At this statement, Rudge slumped to the floor in a faint and it was some time before he could be sufficiently revived for proceedings to continue.

Shedden went on to say that the window shutters were found closed, which he assumed had been done by the intruder to ensure secrecy. It had been at least a month since Rudge had legitimately been in the house, he continued, when he had been seeking the return of a book that he had lent Mr Shedden. However, Mrs Shedden had refused to give back the book since Rudge had spent some money that he had been given to dispose of some pipes. An argument had ensued and Rudge had allegedly threatened the Sheddens. Henry Shedden corroborated his father's evidence.

Next, the inquest heard testimony from Mr Bell, the surgeon, followed by statements from three witnesses who had seen Rudge on the day of the murder. All three were acquainted with Rudge and would easily have recognised him. The first of these was John Reed, who passed the Sheddens' house at around midday on the day of the murder. Reed testified to seeing Rudge and Mrs Shedden in the garden, shaking a carpet. Rudge had removed his jacket and was in his shirtsleeves and, according to Reed, he and the deceased were working 'comfortably'.

William Furze followed Reed. Furze had seen Rudge twice on 20 January, once at eleven o'clock, heading towards Horfield and again at three o'clock, heading back. On the latter occasion, Rudge was not walking fast, but sauntering along nonchalantly with his hands in his pockets. He did not appear to be carrying any weapon.

Finally, Louisa Knight of Clarence Place, Kingsdown, addressed the inquest. The keeper of a beer-house, Louisa testified that Rudge had come into her premises between 2 and 3 o'clock on the day of the murder to buy a pint of beer and a screw of tobacco. According to Mrs Knight, Rudge stayed until almost 10 o'clock at night, leaving frequently, but only for a few minutes at a time. He was cheerful and his clothing appeared normal.

Next to address the inquest was William Butt, assistant overseer of the parish of Horfield, who had accompanied the police when they had arrested Rudge. Butt testified that Rudge had mentioned Mrs Shedden's name in the course of his arrest and that he was positive that nobody had previously spoken the deceased's name in the prisoner's presence. At this, Rudge indicated that he wished to ask a question. Mrs Shedden's name, he maintained, had been first spoken by one of the policemen after Rudge's mother had asked what the matter was. According to Rudge, the policemen had replied, 'Why, Mrs Shedden has been murdered at Horfield' to which Rudge had responded, 'Good God! Mrs Shedden! I'll go with you, for I declare I am innocent.' Both Butt and Rudge insisted that their version of events was correct.

Edward Shakespeare then told the inquest that he too had seen Rudge on the day of the murder, heading towards Bristol between three and four o'clock in the afternoon.

The final witness was Mr William Herepath, an analytical chemist. Herepath had been asked to examine Rudge's clothing and had found what appeared to be four spots of blood on the right leg of his trousers and a further spot on his left bootlace. It was impossible to prove that they were blood unless the garments were subjected to scientific testing, something that had not yet been done.

Having heard all the evidence, the jury returned a verdict of wilful murder against Rudge, who promptly fainted again, recovering a short while later to reaffirm his innocence.

By the time the trial opened at the Spring Assizes at Gloucester on 8 April, the testing of Rudge's clothes had been completed. It was revealed that there were numerous blood spots on his clothes, including some on the inside of his trouser pocket. It was not, however, possible to prove conclusively whether the blood originated from a human being or an animal.

Meanwhile, doubts had been growing about Rudge's involvement in the killing of Mrs Shedden. Not only did he have a solid alibi between midday until 10 o'clock at night, but also evidence had emerged that a number of suspicious people had been seen in the vicinity of the Sheddens' home around the time of the murder. Two men described as 'ballad vendors' had been lurking in the neighbourhood during the weekend prior to the murder and a further man had been seen grinding a lathing hammer at a blacksmith's shop within a few hundred yards of the Sheddens' cottage. His actions and demeanour were described as those of a man who was using the grindstone surreptitiously, by stealth.

The case was heard before Mr Justice Coleridge, with Mr Greaves and Mr Skinner prosecuting and Mr Cripps defending the accused.

The court first heard arguments about the time of Martha Shedden's death. It was her custom to eat dinner at 1 o'clock and, since a pot of water that had boiled dry and contained no potatoes was found over the burnt out ashes of the fire, it was inferred that she had met her death before completing preparations for her dinner.

Witnesses came forward claiming to have seen Rudge running towards Bristol, perspiring heavily, at about one o'clock. Another said he had seen Rudge passing through a gap in a hedge into a field at around three o'clock and, two days after the murder, a silk purse belonging to Mrs Shedden was found in that very field. The question of whether or not Rudge had known the identity of the murder victim before it was officially revealed to him was also addressed, with the same outcome as at the coroner's inquest.

William Herepath was called to the stand to testify about the testing of the prisoner's clothes for blood. He explained that it was not possible to conclusively determine the origin of the blood, human or animal, nor was it possible to establish the age of the bloodstains. Rudge accounted for the presence of blood on his clothes by stating that it could have come from various animals that he had been employed to drive.

Louisa Knight and others repeated their evidence that Rudge had been in Bristol for most of the afternoon and it was pointed out that Rudge himself had admitted to being at the Shedden's home on the day of the murder shaking carpets, but insisted that he had left Martha Shedden alive and well at about ten minutes past twelve. No property belonging to the Sheddens was ever found in his possession.

Then a surprise witness was called. Miss Sowerby, who lived next door to the Sheddens, recalled the milkman calling on the day of the murder. When he knocked at their door, she had looked at her father's watch and noted the time was between seven and eight minutes to three. What is more, she had clearly heard footsteps walking from the Sheddens' parlour to the front door, followed by more footsteps a few minutes later when another person had knocked at the door.

Shedden was recalled to the stand and swore that Miss Sowerby had never mentioned hearing any footsteps to him, but that he thought that she might have discussed them with his son. However, his son also denied having heard about the footsteps, as did Mr Day for the prosecution. It then emerged that fresh footprints had been found near a pool of water at the rear of the cottage and that these could not have been made by the accused.

By this time, questions were being asked in court as to whether there was sufficient evidence against Rudge to proceed. Mr Justice Coleridge observed that, while he could not say that there was no evidence, as the case stood at the present time, he did not feel that he could pass sentence, should the jury find Rudge guilty. He then asked the jury what they thought of the case for the prosecution.

Most of the jury felt that it was unnecessary to continue with the case, but a couple of them stated that they would like to hear a little more evidence. The defence counsel addressed them for a while but the jury seemed to want to hear from the judge himself, so the counsel indicated that he was happy to leave the case in His Lordship's hands.

Mr Justice Coleridge then told the jury that they should ask themselves whether they had heard sufficient evidence to make their decision and, if they had, could he, the judge, then send the accused to the gallows if that decision were for a verdict of guilty? He summarised the evidence, pointing out numerous weaknesses in the prosecution's case and the discrepancies in the testimonies of the witnesses. He addressed the question of whether or not Rudge had named Mrs Shedden, even though her name had not been specifically mentioned, as being quite a natural response – finding the police on his doorstep in connection with the murder of an old lady, it was clear that the only person in his mind would have been the woman he had been working for on that very day.

After a brief deliberation, the jury returned a verdict of not guilty, after which they were told by the counsel for the defence that there were no less than eighteen witnesses who could have given Rudge an alibi for the day of the murder, had it proved necessary.

Rudge was released immediately, but his involvement with the murder of Mrs Shedden did not end there.

He subsequently enlisted in the army and, according to *The Times* of 20 July 1841, it is alleged that he eventually confessed his guilt to one of his comrades in his regiment. His commanding officer wrote to friends of the late Martha Shedden imparting this information, but, having been found not guilty, Rudge was unable to be tried again for the same offence.

6

'IT CANNOT DIE BUT ONCE'

Redcliffe, 1846

In the early hours of the morning of 8 December 1846, PC 200 of the Bristol police force, John Thomas Read, was patrolling his beat in Bath Street. It had been a quiet night until suddenly a fearful scream of 'Murder!' echoed across the river. Read stopped in his tracks and listened intently and, when the scream was almost immediately repeated, he set off in the direction of the noise at a brisk run, crossing Bristol Bridge and arriving in Bridge Street just in time to see a man knocking a woman onto the ground and giving her a heavy kick.

As Read approached, the woman continued to scream hysterically, crying, 'The dear child is dead!' By the light of a nearby street lamp, Read noticed that she was trying to pick something up from the ground and, when he got near enough, he realised that the object was in fact a young baby.

Read took the infant from the woman, straightened its clothes and examined it, telling the couple that the child was 'dying as fast as it could.' The woman was grief stricken but the man seemed almost indifferent, telling the constable, 'It cannot die but once.' By now, a second policeman had arrived on the scene and the two officers arrested the man and took the mother and child to hospital.

Dr Mason examined the infant as soon as she arrived at Bristol General Hospital. He found 10-week-old Anne Elizabeth Cann very cold and unresponsive, with an enormous bruise on the back of her grossly swollen head. He immediately treated her for concussion and 'compression of the brain' but sadly, baby Anne died shortly after five o'clock that morning. Dr Mason later conducted a post-mortem examination, during which he found that a large quantity of blood had leaked between the infant's skull and scalp and that this blood included some brain tissue. There were several separate skull fractures and lacerations to the brain. Mason attributed the death of this otherwise perfectly healthy baby girl to these skull fractures and bleeding, which had evidently occurred as a result of violence.

Bridge Street, Bristol. (Author's collection)

Since the child's mother, Elizabeth Cann, had already told police that her husband, John, had kicked the baby on the head and thrown it three times from one side of the street to the other, this conclusion was hardly surprising.

John and Elizabeth Cann lived in Campbell Terrace, Baptist Mills and Cann worked as a butcher in the family firm at Redcliffe. At 20 years of age, he had recently become a father for the first time when his wife gave birth to their daughter, Anne.

Cann, it seemed, was ill prepared for the realities of becoming a parent and had soon tired of both marriage and fatherhood. Anne's birth had been a bitter disappointment to him, since he had wanted a son rather than a daughter. He was driven almost to distraction by the baby's night-time crying, so much so that he had told his wife that if it didn't stop, he would give the child something to put it to sleep forever. Cann regularly beat both his wife and the baby and he habitually stayed out drinking late at night, often leaving Elizabeth alone in the house with neither money nor food.

An inquest on baby Anne was opened on the day after the fatal attack, before Mr J.B. Grindon, coroner for the city and county of Bristol. It was adjourned later the same day under dramatic circumstances, after the accused suffered an epileptic fit and became so violent in its throes that he had to be subdued by several policemen.

When the inquest was resumed, the jury heard from several witnesses who testified to John Cann's continuous ill-treatment of his daughter. Elizabeth Bird, who lodged at the same house as the Cann family, spoke of hearing the baby screaming and of being told by Mrs Cann that her husband had been blowing smoke into its face. On another occasion, she had heard the child crying and Mrs Cann begging her husband not to hurt the baby. Mrs Bird had rushed upstairs to see what the commotion was about and found Mrs Cann sitting in a chair with the baby in her arms. John Cann had thrown a boot at his wife, which struck her full in the face, causing her nose to bleed profusely. Mrs Cann had thrust the blood-covered baby at Mrs Bird, who had taken it to safety in her room downstairs, all the while hearing Mrs Cann continuing to shout 'Murder!' as her husband beat her.

Another lodger, Mrs Bennett, told the court that, although she had not actually witnessed Cann abusing his daughter, she had seen bruises on the child and been told by Mrs Cann that her husband had caused them. She too had often heard Mrs Cann beg her husband not to beat the child and believed that Cann had disliked his daughter from the moment she was born.

After hearing about Cann's abuse of his baby and the testimony of Dr Mason to the end result of this abuse, not to mention what was almost an eyewitness account from PC Read, the coroner's jury had no hesitation in returning a verdict of 'Wilful Murder.'

The trial opened at the Gloucester Spring Assizes in April 1847. The court heard that, on the day before the fatal attack on his daughter, John Cann had apparently visited a number of pubs and drunk copious amounts of alcohol, although PC Read was later to state that Cann did not appear to be drunk at the time of the offence and that Cann had told him that he had drunk nothing.

More witnesses testified to Cann's prolonged abuse of his daughter. Thomas Strickland, son of the Canns' landlord, told the court that in the month prior to the murder, he had returned home to find Cann beating the child and had been forced to intervene to prevent him from killing her. Elizabeth Cann had been out at the time, but comforted the child when she returned, only for Strickland to hear it screaming loudly again later that same day. The next-door neighbours had also witnessed Cann maltreating the baby.

John Pearce and his wife Catherine took the stand to testify about Cann's relationship with the child. Mrs Pearce stated that she had never heard Cann say anything particular about the baby but that she had seen bruising on the child, which she described as looking like the marks of knuckles. During Catherine Pearce's testimony, John Cann was suddenly stricken by another serious seizure, but was assisted by the doctors who were present in court to give their evidence and was soon pronounced well enough for the trial to proceed.

Mr Pearce, who worked with Cann at his butcher's shop, gave exactly the same evidence as his wife, but was immediately cautioned by the judge to the effect that he had already given a different sworn statement. Pearce then admitted that he had heard Cann say that he disliked his wife and child and that Cann had told him that his father had offered him money if he would leave them.

Mr Mason, the surgeon who had treated baby Anne and subsequently performed her post-mortem examination, was then recalled to the witness stand and questioned about Cann's epilepsy. Mason told the court that, after having a fit, a person might do things without knowing what he was doing. On some occasions, recovery might be quicker than on others.

Crucially, John Cann had had an epileptic seizure on the night of the murder, just thirty minutes before allegedly beating his wife and killing his child. When taken to the police station after the incident, he had been calm and rational but

The General Hospital at the turn of the twentieth century. (Author's collection)

had stated that he 'did not know what he was about.' He had asked William Harris, the custody officer, what time he would be taken before the magistrates and what Harris thought his fate would be.

Was Cann's epilepsy reason enough to be considered an extenuating circumstance in the murder of his daughter? Apparently, the jury believed that it was as, after deliberating for a short time, they found Cann not guilty of murder, but guilty of manslaughter.

The judge, Mr Gaselee, then addressed Cann, telling him, 'A more diabolical crime than yours I have scarcely ever had before me.' He told Cann that he believed that the jury had reached the proper conclusion but said that, had they found him guilty of murder, then he doubted that anyone would have intervened to save his life. Gaselee continued by saying that it was quite clear to him that Cann had acted with deliberate intention to destroy his child and pointed out that it would not do for anyone who was subject to epileptic fits to think that they could commit offences and get away without punishment simply on account of their medical condition. With that, he sentenced John Cann to be transported for life.

[Note: There are some variations in contemporary accounts of the murder by John Cann. His daughter's name is variously spelled Ann and Anne; also, on occasions, is given as Elizabeth Anne rather than Anne Elizabeth. The first police officer to arrive on the scene is named as both John Thomas Read and John Thomas Lee. The most frequently used names have been selected for this chapter.]

7

'YOU MUST HAVE THOUGHT WE WERE KILLING EACH OTHER'

St Augustines, 1849

Shortly after five o'clock on the morning of 3 March 1849, Mrs Isabella Fry woke suddenly to the sound of screams. Within moments her lodger, Mrs Anne Ham, had also been disturbed by the blood-curdling sounds. The two women agreed that the noise seemed to be coming from the house next door, 6 Trenchard Street, specifically from the bedroom where their neighbour and landlady, Elizabeth Jeffries, normally slept. At Mrs Fry's suggestion, Mrs Ham banged on the dividing wall with her walking stick and, as she did, the noise stopped abruptly, leaving the ladies to finish their sleep in peace.

Barely two hours later, there was a knock at the door. Mrs Ham answered, and on the doorstep stood a young girl, who introduced herself as Miss Jeffries's maid. Sarah Thomas said that she had been sent to apologise for the disturbance, explaining that a cat had jumped onto her mistress's bed, frightening her half to death. 'You must have thought we were killing each other' she joked. Mrs Ham was disbelieving. 'It was no cat', she argued, telling the maid that she had heard her crying in the yard before and thought that she had been making the noise because her mistress was trying to pull her out of bed. Sarah denied this, although she did confide that Miss Jeffries was 'such a good for nothing woman' that she couldn't live with her.

Sarah Harriet Thomas was, it seemed, the latest of numerous servants employed by Miss Jeffries, a woman who was so unpleasant that she rarely received any visitors and whose own brother deliberately gave her a wide berth. However, the elderly lady did have one friend, a Mrs Susan Miller. Mrs Miller had called at the house to see Miss Jeffries on the previous afternoon and had promised to return that day. However, when she did return, no amount of knocking at the door elicited any response from within – the house appeared shut up and empty.

Trenchard Street – now the site of a multi-storey car park. (©N. Sly)

Earlier that morning, it had been a different matter. A neighbour who lived across the street had watched Sarah and a male companion removing items from the house, eventually walking off together carrying a bundle.

This bundle was left at a confectioner's shop in nearby Maudlin Lane, to be called for later that day. Sarah unexpectedly turned up at the home of her parents, George and Ann Thomas, in Horfield. Her parents asked no questions as she carried her luggage into the house, leaving shortly afterwards to return to Bristol to collect her bundle and returning at around half past nine in the evening.

Sarah spent the next day with her parents, who were surprisingly reticent in asking her about the jewellery, money and silverware that had come home with her. Still, it was not the first time that Sarah had suddenly left her job and neither was it the first time that money and trinkets had left with her.

On Wednesday 7 March, the body of Miss Jeffries was found lying in her bedroom with numerous wounds to her head; her pillow and bolster completely soaked with blood. The room was in some disarray and indeed, the whole house appeared to have been ransacked. The first persons to gain entry to the house included Miss Jeffries's brother, Henry, himself a retired surgeon, who quickly surmised that his sister had died from violence. Nearby lay a large stone, weighing around 4lbs, which was usually used as a doorstop and which bore traces of grey hair and clotted blood. The body of Miss Jeffries's dog, which was known to always bark at strangers, was found in the backyard privy.

Mr Ralph Bernard, a surgeon, later carried out a post-mortem examination and concluded that Miss Jeffries had died of concussion and compression of the brain. She had three contused wounds on the left-hand side of her forehead, and a 2in wound on the top of her head. Just to the right of this was a slightly smaller Y-shaped wound and there were numerous other contusions and skin abrasions, including one on her left hand. This, along with Miss Jeffries's position in the bed, which gave the impression that she was trying to get up at the time of her death, suggested that she may have attempted to defend herself against her attacker. The injuries had been caused by a blunt instrument and a closer examination of the large stone showed that it fitted the wounds exactly.

Police immediately set off in pursuit of the missing maid, their first port of call being her parents' cottage. Sarah's mother initially denied that her daughter was at home but the officers insisted on looking round anyway, eventually finding Sarah crouched, partially dressed, under the stairs in the coal-hole. A thorough search of the cottage revealed all sorts of treasures – jewellery, including a gold chain, foreign coins, twenty-seven sovereigns, four half-sovereigns and a quantity of silver and copper coins. Most damning were four shifts, each marked with the initials 'E.J.' and a petticoat belonging to Sarah, which bore bloodstains. Sarah was promptly arrested, as was her mother. When searched at the police station after her arrest, Sarah was found to have five silver teaspoons concealed in her stocking, all engraved with the letters 'E.J.'

Initially, Sarah tried to lay the blame for her employer's death on Miss Jeffries's brother. Then, she abruptly changed her story, telling the police that a girl who said she was a former servant had arrived at the house on the Saturday morning, demanding a word with Miss Jeffries.

The visitor told Sarah that she was having problems obtaining references from her previous employer and had picked up the large stone from beside the kitchen door and gone upstairs to Miss Jeffries's bedroom, obviously with the intention of persuading her to co-operate. Sarah told police that she had gone up to the bedroom a little later and seen the elderly lady lying folded in her bedclothes. The former servant had given Sarah the money and jewellery as an inducement not to tell and told her to leave, promising to lock up after her. The girl's name, Sarah recalled, was either Maria Lewis or Maria Williams.

Strenuous efforts were made to identify the mysterious Maria. Susan Miller vaguely remembered a servant employed by her friend in the recent past, but believed that girl's name to be Rebecca. The proprietors of domestic staffing agencies (known as intelligence offices) were quizzed at length, but nobody could identify the young maid that Sarah swore had killed her mistress.

The last known servant of Miss Jeffries, prior to Sarah's appointment, was 16-year-old Lucy Chad. Lucy had had health problems but, having recovered, had travelled to Bristol to live with her aunt in Avon Street while looking for work. She was engaged by Miss Jeffries but spent only five weeks in her situation before she suffered a relapse, mainly, she claimed, due to the unkind treatment she received from her employer. Lucy also maintained that her mistress had always carefully locked the house every night and slept with the keys in her bedroom – if this was so, how could Sarah have opened the door to admit Maria?

Yet Lucy had left Trenchard Street on 24 January and Sarah Thomas didn't begin work until 5 February. This left a period of two weeks during which the mysterious Maria or Rebecca could have been in service to Miss Jeffries. One firm did recall supplying a servant for Miss Jeffries in early January but could

Above: *Host Street, early 1900s. The Flitch of Bacon is on the extreme left of the picture. (Author's collection)*

Left: *Host Street, 2007. (©N. Sly)*

not give her name. Miss Jeffries had dismissed this girl as unsatisfactory on account of her being too dozy and for wearing too many flounces on her gown. Another intelligence office recalled sending several servants for Miss Jeffries's approval during the week commencing 22 January. However, an inspection of the agency books showed that none of the girls' names had been recorded and none had been hired.

Then a new witness came forward, a 9-year-old girl called Mary Ann Sullivan. Mary Ann's uncle, John Collins, was a fiddler who played at the local pubs to supplement the relief money he received from the parish. He was blind and it was her job to lead him from pub to pub. Mary Ann knew Sarah Thomas quite well and told police that Sarah had been courting a rifleman for at least a month prior to the murder.

On the Saturday of the murder, Mary Ann claimed to have been in the Flitch of Bacon public house in Host Street with her uncle. There she had seen a young man whom she knew as Matthew Lyon, in the company of two riflemen, one of whom was Sarah's boyfriend. Mary claimed to have eavesdropped as the three men plotted the murder of Mrs Jeffries. According to Mary Ann, she had watched the three men climb over the wall separating the pub from Mrs Jeffries's yard at around midnight. She had then followed them through a door in the wall to see Lyon strike the elderly woman on the forehead, while one of the riflemen hit her with the side of his sword. Lyon had then killed the dog and thrown it into the yard.

Again, we must question why the men would climb a 20ft wall to gain access to Miss Jeffries's house if they could have simply walked through a door? The landlady of the pub denied knowing Mary Ann Sullivan but hinted that the girl came from a bad lot and was 'not quite in her senses'. Nevertheless, the keys to Miss Jeffries's home were found in a groove in a windowsill of the Flitch of Bacon on the very day that Mrs Jeffries's body was discovered. Had they lain there unnoticed since the murder or been placed there at a later date?

At the coroner's investigation into the murder, Mary Ann was accused of telling lies and threatened with punishment if she continued to do so. If her evidence was the truth, admonished the coroner, then she had nothing to fear but if she had lied, then she had better confess at once. Mary Ann insisted that she was telling the truth and signed her deposition accordingly. As it was being read to the court, Sarah Thomas laughed out loud several times.

In his summary of the facts for the jury, the coroner, Mr J.B. Grindon, discounted Mary Ann Sullivan's evidence as 'wholly unworthy of credit.' He told the jury that they would have to rely largely on circumstantial evidence in reaching their verdict, but that, in his opinion, the evidence was strong and appeared to point to Sarah Thomas alone as the murderess. The jury retired for fifteen minutes before returning with a verdict of wilful murder against Sarah Harriet Thomas.

At this, all traces of Sarah's former levity vanished and she burst into noisy tears, burying her face in her handkerchief. It seemed as if all her strength deserted her, since she had to be assisted from the court 'hanging like a dead weight on the arms of the policemen.' Outside the court, a large, angry crowd of people had gathered to hear the coroner's ruling and police had to struggle to protect Sarah from them as she was transported to gaol to await her forthcoming trial at the Gloucester Assizes.

The trial opened on 3 April, before Mr Baron Platt, with Mr Whitmore and Mr Skinner as counsel for the prosecution and Mr Serjeant Allen appearing for the defence. First the court heard the circumstances of the discovery of Miss Jeffries's body. Next came the statements from Miss Jeffries's next door neighbours, her brother and Mr Bernard, the police surgeon.

Numerous witnesses mentioned Miss Jeffries's character. She was described as not having an amiable disposition and as being a violent woman who was known to ill-treat her servants. Mrs Ham testified to hearing her neighbour call Sarah Thomas a 'dirty hussy' and complaining loudly that she was slow at her work. Lucy Chad and other previous servants spoke of being threatened with beatings, particularly when Miss Jeffries, who insisted that her servants rise at five o'clock every morning, considered that they hadn't got out of bed quickly or early enough.

Counsel for the defence did not dispute any of the facts put forward by the prosecution, but did dispute the inferences drawn from them. He did not deny that Miss Jeffries had met her death by his client's hand, nor that she had lied about her part in the murder, but did deny that Sarah Thomas had committed a premeditated murder with the intention of afterwards robbing her mistress. If that were the case, he maintained, then Thomas would have selected a more appropriate weapon and made better preparations for her escape. A hatchet, a poker, a hammer, several knives and other instruments of death had been readily available to her, some even in the bedroom where the killing occurred. A stone was the last weapon a cold-blooded, calculating killer would have chosen.

The clothes that Miss Jeffries was wearing when her body was discovered were not strictly nightclothes, indicating that she had already been up and about on the morning of her death. The screams heard by the neighbours were, according to their testimony, similar to the sounds of crying that they had heard Sarah Thomas make in the past.

Miss Jeffries was not in the habit of rising before ten or eleven o'clock in the morning, yet her servants had to be up at five. And it was shortly after five o'clock in the morning that neighbours reported hearing the sound of screaming coming from next door.

Mr Serjeant Allen asked the jury, was it not more probable that the deceased had risen from her bed to force Sarah Thomas to get up? That the two women had quarrelled and that Sarah had inflicted the fatal blows 'in a moment of rage, passion and ungovernable fury?' If the jury found Thomas guilty of murder, then her life would be sacrificed. At very least, there was sufficient doubt that there was any suggestion of malice aforethought and, in that case, the charge should be reduced to manslaughter. The defence counsel then reminded the jury that they would have to live with the consequences of their decision for the rest of their lives. Sarah wept continuously while her counsel spoke, showing her first signs of any emotion in the entire proceedings.

In summing up, the judge cautioned the jury against being led away from the facts of the case by what he called 'this strong, eloquent and pathetic appeal', while reminding them that if they had any doubts as to Sarah Thomas's guilt, they should give her the benefit of this doubt.

Sarah Harriet Thomas. (By kind permission of Bristol Central Library)

The jury retired, leaving just enough time for a charge of horse-stealing to be heard in their absence. In the course of this hearing, some amusing evidence was put forward, causing a good deal of laughter in the court, with Sarah Thomas laughing as heartily as anyone else.

When the jury returned after thirty minutes' deliberation, they announced a verdict of guilty, but with a recommendation for mercy on the grounds of the defendant's youth. Thomas showed no emotion at the verdict, but when the judge put on his black cap, she buried her face in her hands saying, 'Oh, I cannot stand that.'

In passing sentence of death, the judge said that he saw no reason for the jury's recommendation to be considered, although he promised to forward their concerns to the proper quarter. As a gaoler came to take Thomas after sentence was pronounced, she begged him to ask the judge to spare her life, saying that she would not leave the court until he had done so. A second gaoler was forced to assist in removing her and her sobbing as she left court affected many of those in attendance.

In the event, the recommendation for mercy came to nothing and Sarah Thomas was hanged at Bristol Prison on 20 April 1849. Her age at the time of her death was variously given as 17 and 19 years old.

[Note: In different contemporary accounts of the murder, there is some variation of names. Mrs Fry, who heard screaming from next door is referred to as either Isabella or Jane, while Susan Miller, friend of the deceased, is also referred to as Sarah.]

8

'SO HELP ME GOD, IT SHALL BE EITHER FOR LIFE OR DEATH THIS NIGHT'

St Philips, 1852

Thirty-two-year-old Elizabeth Spear was a clean, conscientious woman, a mother of four children, who often took in work at home to help make ends meet. Unfortunately, Elizabeth was married to a rather feckless man who worked as a shoemaker, when he could be bothered to turn up for work rather than spending his time and money on a perpetual pub crawl.

Tuesday 19 October 1852 was one of those days when John Spear couldn't be bothered. In the company of his brother, Abraham, who was also a married man, he began his day's drinking at 9 a.m. By lunchtime, he had spent all his money, but managed to persuade his brother to pawn his coat. The cash from this transaction bought the brother's drinks until 3 p.m., when John's pockets were once again empty and he was forced to return home to try and wheedle some more money from his long-suffering wife.

Elizabeth angrily told him that she had no money, then left him sulking at home while she went to visit a sick child in hospital. When she got back, there was no trace of John – and neither was there any trace of her two good dresses, which John had taken to the pawnshop. The dresses had fetched the princely sum of 6*s* – more than enough money to buy a few more rounds of drinks for the two brothers.

Furious, Elizabeth picked up her youngest child and went round to see her sister-in-law. Together, the two women went off to look for their missing husbands, in the company of a female friend.

The drinkers were finally located at the Old Castle Tavern, on Castle Street. Handing the baby to her friend, Elizabeth marched over to her husband and began to give him a piece of her mind about his drinking and the missing dresses, calling him a 'scamp' and finishing her tirade with the words, 'So help me God, it shall be either for life or death this night.'

Having sat quietly and listened to his wife's outburst, John Spear called for a fresh pint of Burton beer. Elizabeth was outraged. 'If you have any more Burton,' she threatened, 'I'll break the pint over your head.' With that, she grabbed a smoking pipe from a nearby table and flung it at him, hitting him hard on the forehead. She then called for three pennyworth of rum and went to stand in front of the fireplace.

Before her drink could arrive, John Spear got up without saying a word and took a few steps towards his wife, who promptly crumpled to the floor. He then sat down again at another table. At first, the other patrons at the pub believed that Elizabeth had either fainted or suffered an attack of apoplexy. Then someone noticed blood seeping from beneath her clothes and pooling on the floor of the inn. 'Go and fetch a doctor, for I know what I have done', demanded Spear.

A doctor was immediately sent for, but by the time surgeon Mr James Leaker arrived, he was too late to do anything more than pronounce Elizabeth Spear dead. At a later post-mortem examination, Mr Bernard, surgeon to the police force, was to discover a puncture wound in Elizabeth's pelvis, which had severed her iliac artery, causing almost 4lbs of blood to leak into her abdominal cavity. The only outward sign of the fatal injury was a small wound around three-quarters of an inch in length, but death would have been almost instantaneous due to loss of blood. The post-mortem also confirmed that Elizabeth had been pregnant with her fifth child.

Police found a bloodstained knife under the seat where John Spear had sat after his wife had fallen. It was a clasp knife, with a pointed blade between 3in and 4in long, with a spring at the back to keep it open. When Mr Bernard tried to push the knife through the holes in Elizabeth Spear's clothing, it fitted exactly.

The pub had been crowded and there had been numerous witnesses to the incident. However, beyond hearing John being 'bullied' by Elizabeth Spear, few of them seemed to have seen anything. Some of them had seen Spear 'brush past' his wife before she fell; some had seen him push her. Others had seen him driving his fist into her bowels or her side, but nobody had seen a knife in his hand or even realised that Elizabeth was mortally wounded.

At the inquest into the death of Elizabeth Spear, the coroner, Mr J.B. Grindon, instructed the jury that the fact that Spear had been drinking all day aggravated rather than excused his actions. It was his opinion, Grindon told the jury, that the main factor that they needed to consider in reaching their verdict was whether or not Spear had been sufficiently provoked by his wife to reduce the charges against him from murder to manslaughter. Grindon pointed out that any provocation had come when Elizabeth first entered the public house and addressed her husband. Since Elizabeth had finished berating her husband and had moved away from him to a different part of the inn when she was stabbed, then the relevance of the provocation had passed. The coroner felt that there could have been no intention in Spear's stabbing of his wife other than to cause a mortal injury. Thus, to return a verdict of anything less than wilful murder would be little short of encouragement to crime.

The jury heeded his comments and returned a verdict of wilful murder against John Spear, who was committed for trial at the next assizes at Gloucester. There he obviously met with a more sympathetic jury, since he avoided the death penalty, instead being transported for life. The fate of his four young children is unknown.

9

'IT'S NO STRANGER
DID THAT'

Hotwells / Clifton, 1855

In 1855, well before the completion of Brunel's famous suspension bridge, there was a cliffside quarry on the Hotwells side of the Avon Gorge. Nearby was a cluster of tiny cottages, built for the quarry workers and a little further up the Gorge, on the edge of Clifton Downs, was Cook's Folly tavern, an alehouse known for its stock of fine quality beers.

It was here that 9-year-old Melinda Payne was sent on an errand by her mother to fetch some beer for her father, a carpenter at the quarry. It was a trip that the girl had made several times before and should have been a pleasant hour's walk on a balmy August evening. Wearing a brown dress covered by a coarse white pinafore, with a garden bonnet on her head, Melinda set off at about 6 p.m., carrying a ginger ale bottle to collect the beer and tightly clutching a sixpence with which to pay for it.

Shortly after she set off on her errand, Melinda bumped into her older brother, 12-year-old George, on his way home from work. She asked him for a halfpenny so that she could buy some biscuits at the inn.

George continued home and reported that he had met his sister. When Melinda didn't return at the expected time, George was sent to look for her. He walked as far as the alehouse where the landlady, Mary Ann O'Connor, told him that Melinda had already collected the beer some time before and been given two little cakes.

George rushed home, arriving at about 8 p.m., fully expecting to find his little sister waiting for him, but she was not there. Leaving Melinda's mother behind with the youngest two of her five children, Melinda's father and her two oldest siblings collected lanterns and candles and went out to search for the missing child. They could find no trace of her.

The search party returned home briefly at about 10 p.m., by which time Melinda's frantic mother could bear to wait no longer. Afraid that her daughter may have fallen and hurt herself, she insisted that the family went out again, joining them in their search until 4 a.m. At this time, when there was still no news

35

View of Cook's Folly, Clifton Downs. (Author's collection)

of the missing child, the Paynes' lodger was roused from his bed and willingly went out with Mr Payne, who had not slept at all night, to continue combing the countryside.

In the event, it was George Payne who found the body of his sister at just after 7 a.m. on the morning after she had disappeared. Melinda lay in a rocky hollow at the rear of a cottage where labourer Samuel Handy lived with his wife, Elizabeth and their children. The body, which had been partially covered with rocks in an attempt to conceal it, lay with one arm raised as if to ward off an attack. Melinda's face was covered with blood, which had originated from dreadful injuries to her head and knife wounds to her throat. Nearby lay the broken remains of the two cakes she had been given, but there was no trace of the full beer flagon she had been carrying.

The police were called and Inspector Attwood took charge of the case. His first task was to order the body to be removed to a nearby pub pending the inquest, which opened the very next day at the Rownham tavern before coroner Mr J.B. Grindon.

The first person to give evidence was Mr Crosby Leonard, a surgeon who had made a post-mortem examination on the body of the dead child. Leonard described the extensive signs of violence he had observed to Melinda's face, head, throat, thighs and one of her arms. The most serious of her injuries were two head wounds. Although less than an inch in length, one wound had a corresponding skull fracture through which part of the child's brain protruded. Melinda also had a second skull fracture, this one being 13in long. She had a broken jaw and her throat had also been slashed. The cut across her throat was 3½in in length but had miraculously failed to damage any major blood vessels or her windpipe.

Leonard theorised that the wounds might have been caused by more than one weapon. Either a blow or a fall would have caused the large skull fracture and the broken jaw, while a sharp instrument such as a common knife had made the other wounds. According to Mr Leonard, the cause of Melinda's death had been the severe injuries to her brain, although he could not say whether those injuries were deliberately inflicted or whether they occurred as a result of a fall or accident. The cuts, however, were a different matter as Leonard could state quite categorically that they had been intentionally inflicted. Finally, he was able to determine that Melinda had not been sexually assaulted.

Next to give evidence before the inquest was Melinda's brother, George, who was described in the newspapers of the time as 'an intelligent lad'. George recounted meeting with his sister as she went off on her errand and of later going out and searching for her when she failed to return home. He also described his gruesome discovery early the following morning.

The final witness of the day was Inspector Attwood, who had a shocking revelation to impart. In a routine search of the Payne family home, police had found some bloodstained clothes belonging to Melinda's father. At this, the coroner adjourned the inquest to allow the police more time to investigate.

When it reopened, the police had managed to establish that there was an innocent explanation for the bloody clothing. Having questioned James Payne, they discovered that he had had an accident at work on the day before the murder. According to his wife, Sarah, on the day Melinda was killed, her husband had come home from work, taken off his shoes and taken the baby from her, nursing it and keeping it amused while she went about the housework. He had continuously nursed the child from 6 p.m. to 8 p.m., when George had arrived home and reported that he had not located his missing sister. James had then put on his shoes again and gone out to search. William Skinner, the Paynes' lodger, confirmed that James Payne had spent the entire evening at home, up until leaving to begin the search for his daughter.

None of the Handy family, whose garden was close to where the child's body had been found, reported hearing or seeing anything unusual on the night of the murder. Given the extent of Melinda's injuries, it was thought that she had struggled and fought her killer, leading the police to believe that she had been attacked elsewhere and her body dumped in the hollow and covered with rocks in an attempt to conceal it from view. This scenario was supported by the discovery of a bloodstained knife by a young boy, Charles Lovering. The knife had been discarded in a drain hole on the path from Clifton to Hotwells that Melinda would have taken. The ginger ale bottle that she was carrying was eventually found in woods some 50yds away. The bottle had been partially concealed by stones, one of which bore bloodstains.

Even though the Handy family had neither seen nor heard a struggle, they did provide the investigating officers with one important piece of information. Both Mr and Mrs Handy separately gave statements to the police in which they maintained that they had seen Melinda's father, James Payne, walking alone along the gully behind their home. Both put the time of this sighting as between 6 p.m. and 7 p.m. – much earlier than 8 p.m., when Payne's family had stated that he went out searching for the first time. When a member of the coroner's jury asked

Cook's Folly, Bristol. (Author's collection)

whether there was anyone who could independently corroborate this sighting, Inspector Attwood assured him that there was such a witness, but that she had refused to attend the inquest unless she was summoned to do so. The coroner told the jury that there would be no difficulty in issuing a summons for the attendance of this witness if it were necessary, but at that time he didn't feel that it was.

Apart from Mary Ann O'Connor, the landlady of the alehouse that Melinda had visited, only one other person was traced who believed he had seen Melinda on the night of her murder. This was Thomas King, a young donkey driver, who had been out with his donkey carriage and seen a girl matching Melinda's description at about 6.45 p.m. walking from the direction of Cook's Folly. Later that same evening, he had been returning his donkeys to their pasture in the company of some other boys when he met James Payne together with two of his children, out searching for the missing girl. Payne had, at that time, offered King some money if he managed to find the child. King had initially told Payne that he had spoken to his daughter earlier that evening. However, when he gave evidence at the inquest, King stated that he hadn't spoken to her.

The eventual verdict of the coroner's inquest was 'wilful murder by person or persons unknown'. The newspapers of the time reported that police had sought extra help from other officers 'of great experience in such matters'. Whether or not these were local policemen or officers from Scotland Yard is not made clear, but regardless of the extra manpower, police seemed no closer to identifying the killer of Melinda Payne. In September, the then Secretary of State, Sir G. Grey, offered a reward, in response to an appeal by the mayor of Bristol. The government agreed to pay the sum of 100s for information leading to the conviction of the murderer and to recommend a pardon to any accomplice, not being the person who actually committed the murder, who gave such information.

Even this substantial reward failed to elicit anything to bring the police any closer to identifying Melinda's murderer. James Payne had remarked that, 'It's no stranger did that' and, indeed, there were no reports of any strangers in the area on the night of the murder. Yet, the investigation raises some questions, to which satisfactory answers have never been found.

Mr and Mrs Handy were quite certain that they had seen James Payne out in the area alone, well before he was supposed to have started searching for his daughter. Who was the missing witness who, if called, might have corroborated their statements? Was the blood on Payne's shirt solely down to his work accident? His lodger, William Skinner, confirmed his alibi for the time of the murder. Yet Skinner himself left the house shortly after 7 o'clock that evening to make a trip to Bristol. Did Payne's family close ranks to provide him with an alibi and protect him?

If Payne did murder his daughter, what was his motive? In fact, what was anyone's motive for killing an innocent young girl? She was not sexually assaulted and she had no money or other possessions to be stolen – could it be that Melinda Payne was killed for nothing more than a quart of beer?

The case remains unsolved to this day.

10

'OH NO, A CHILD COULD PLAY WITH IT'

Leigh Woods, 1857

On 11 September 1857, at about seven o'clock in the evening, gamekeeper George Worts was going about his normal daily routine on the estate of Leigh Court, situated close to the foot of the Clifton Suspension Bridge. In Nightingale Valley, he spotted what he believed to be a patch of blood, which somebody had evidently tried to conceal by kicking soil over it. Looking around, he noticed footprints, which he followed until he saw what appeared to be the body of a woman lying in a crumpled heap about 12ft below a large, overhanging rock. He rushed to Ashton police station for assistance, returning with Superintendent Jones. Between them, the men retrieved the body and it was taken to the nearby New Inn at Rownham Ferry to await an inquest.

The woman, her identity then unknown, had been shot in the right-hand side of her head and her throat bore two slash marks that were so deep that she was almost decapitated. Animals had torn away parts of her throat.

She was described as between 20 and 30 years of age, of diminutive stature and rather handsome, and was dressed in a dark grey dress trimmed with white lace. One pocket had been cut away from the dress. Near to the body lay a bloody, lace-trimmed handkerchief embroidered with the initials 'C.P.'

As the county coroner, Mr B. Fry, lived some distance away, it took several days to arrange for a post-mortem examination. Meanwhile, the police made exhaustive efforts to identify the body.

At first it looked as though it would not be too difficult to name the young woman as, almost immediately after the news of the murder broke, a local innkeeper, Mrs Bowden came forward. She told police that a woman dressed in a similar grey outfit to the deceased had come into her inn in the company of a sailor. She remembered them particularly because they had asked for Devonshire cider, but had not liked the drink and had eventually exchanged it for beer. The woman had paid for the drink, taking some money from a purse that was brimming with sovereigns.

Above: *Clifton Suspension Bridge and Leigh Woods. (Author's collection)*

Right: *Nightingale Valley. (Author's collection)*

Rownham Ferry. The New Inn is the white building to the left of the picture. (Author's collection)

Mrs Bowden had engaged the woman in conversation and learned that she had come to Bristol from Hull and was on her way to Appledore in Devon to meet her husband, the captain and owner of a timber ship that had just docked from Quebec. It so happened that Mrs Bowden was herself a native of Appledore and was able to give the young woman details of a place where she might lodge. Having established that the sailor was only an acquaintance who was accompanying her on her journey, the innkeeper cautioned her customer about displaying her money so freely. The young woman reassured Mrs Bowden that the man had been very kind to her.

The two women discussed the grey alpaca dress, which the captain's wife said was very comfortable for travelling. She then went on to tell Mrs Bowden that she and her companion intended to spend the afternoon in Leigh Woods and to see the suspension bridge. She promised to call back at the inn on her way to catch her train, but never returned.

When the body was found in Leigh Woods, Mrs Bowden and another woman, who had been in the pub at the time, both felt that the description of the dress worn by the deceased sounded remarkably similar to that worn by the sea captain's wife. They contacted the police and Mrs Bowden was taken to view the body. The dead woman's face was too discoloured to allow Mrs Bowden to make a positive identification, although she felt that the dress was identical in appearance to that of her customer.

Hopes of an early identification of the body were dashed the following morning when, as a result of police enquiries, the captain's wife was found alive and well at

Appledore. Another pub landlady, Mrs Caroline Green of the White Lion, Temple Street, told police that she believed that the woman could have recently lodged at her inn, again in the company of a sailor. Both Mrs Green and her servant viewed the body and both were positive that it was their lodger, who had told them that she had been fetched from her job in service at Clevedon by her husband and that they were going on to London, where his mother was going to set them up in business. Mrs Green recalled the woman saying that her own mother lived in Hotwell Road, Bristol, and police immediately began enquiries to try and find anyone who had recently left her job under the circumstances described.

A photograph was taken of the dead girl and handbills were printed and circulated. A plaster cast was also made of the head, but by this time the body had begun to decompose and it was felt that, rather than assisting in identifying the young woman, the cast would prove a hindrance. Hundreds of people flocked to see the body when it was placed on display, but to no avail. Miss C.P. – if those were indeed her initials – remained unidentified.

Eventually police looked to the dead woman's undergarments for further clues and found that her stays had been manufactured by Goodmans of Stall Street, Bath. A visit to the retailer elicited the information that the stays had been purchased by a young woman, who had told them that she was soon to be married and that she and her husband intended to emigrate to America. Then, laundry marks on the underwear were recognised by a laundress who had worked for the Honourable Mrs Hutchinson at Dorset House, Clifton. Mary Ann Kelston, a dressmaker eventually identified the dead woman's dress as her own work and Mr Burt, a shoemaker from Bath, was able to identify a repair to the boots that the dead woman was wearing as having been carried out by him. All identified the wearer of the clothes as Charlotte Pugsley.

These clues eventually led police to Hill House, the home of Samuel Bythsea in Freshford, near Bath, where, until the previous week, Charlotte had worked for three months as head cook. Then she had given notice, telling her employer that she was soon to marry. She withdrew her savings from the Bath Savings Bank and eventually left Freshford with her husband-to-be, John William Beale, on the evening of 9 September, seemingly under the impression that they were going to Southampton to be married, before sailing to America.

Beale was employed as a butler at Badbey House, Daventry, but on 6 September had requested compassionate leave from his employer, Captain Watkins, on account of a serious accident to his father. According to Beale, when the news of his father's accident had been brought to his home, his younger sister had been so affected that she had collapsed from shock and later died. Beale was a married man, who had met Charlotte when they had both worked at Dorset House. When Mrs Hutchinson, their employer, left Clifton to live in Ireland, Charlotte had moved in with Beale and his wife, but Mrs Beale had been jealous and Charlotte was forced to move out rather hurriedly. She had taken up a new position at Freshford, where it seems Beale often visited her, almost certainly without telling his wife!

Beale had arrived at Wine Street, Bristol, on Monday 7 September, calling in at Aplin's tailor's shop where his cousin worked. During his visit to the shop, Beale had asked to be measured for a new coat and it was noted that he carried a small pistol in his breast pocket. When warned by the tailor of the dangers of carrying a loaded pistol, Beale dismissed his concerns, saying, 'Oh no, a child could play with it.' For two days he remained in Bristol, drinking and playing bagatelle with his cousin and his cousin's workmates in the King's Head tavern in Wine Street and ordering a new hat from a shop in Clare Street. On the Wednesday, he had told his cousin that he was off to visit Bath, arriving at Freshford that afternoon. He had collected Charlotte and the three large bags containing her belongings, depositing the bags at Limpley Stoke station to be collected at a later date. He then returned to Bristol with Charlotte and was seen in the city by several acquaintances on the following day, each time accompanied by a woman matching Charlotte's description. He collected his new hat at about 1 o'clock on Saturday 12 September.

When a fellow servant of Charlotte Pugsley travelled from Bath to Bristol and positively identified her clothes, including a pair of stockings that she had personally mended for the deceased, police immediately circulated a description of John Beale. It was printed in *The Times* as:

About 30 years old, 5 feet 4 or 5 inches high, slight make, thin face, pale complexion, hair nearly black, worn long, and turned under at the back of the head, small black whiskers, dark eyes, good teeth, dressed in black frock jacket, with pocket outside the left breast, double-breasted black waistcoat and black or shepherd's plaid trousers made very large at the feet. He is flat-footed, has an awkward gait and turns his feet out very much when walking. He wore an old-fashioned silver watch and massive silver Albert chain and a ring set with red stones on the little finger. He has been a butler or single-handed servant in gentlemen's families and is supposed to have recently come from Daventry, near Northampton. He is well known in Bristol and the neighbourhoods of Clifton and Bath.

The Home Secretary authorised a reward of 100s for information leading to his capture, with a free pardon for any accomplice not being the actual perpetrator of the crime.

The fugitive was not at large for long, being apprehended at Daventry within days. Bristol police were notified of his capture by electric telegraph and Inspector Norris of the Bath police escorted him to Bristol by train. On his arrival, on the evening of 25 September, he was immediately taken before magistrates at Bourton Union workhouse. He gave a statement to the police admitting to meeting Charlotte at Freshford, but alleging that she was a married woman who went by her maiden name of Pugsley. He had escorted her to Bristol and handed her over to her husband, a man whose surname he didn't know, but whose Christian name was either George or Thomas. He was to have met with the couple the following day, but they hadn't turned up, so Beale had returned to his job at Daventry, taking Charlotte's luggage with him in the hope that she would arrange to collect it. However, he had told his colleagues that the boxes belonged to his sister, whose funeral he had applied for compassionate leave to attend.

Beale was charged with the wilful murder of Charlotte Pugsley and remanded at the Bourton Union workhouse until the following day, when he was again brought before magistrates. The chairman, the Revd Henry Morehouse, expressed concern that Beale was not defended. When he asked the prisoner if he would wish to be defended, Beale concurred that he would, so Morehouse proposed that he would only deal with items of evidence that were undisputed, that no counsel or solicitor in the world would attempt to disprove. Accordingly, magistrates heard only that the body of a woman had been discovered, the medical evidence on how she died and the evidence of the witnesses who would state what had happened at Daventry. Beale was given the opportunity to question the witnesses.

First came the evidence of Geroge Worts, who had found Pugsley's body. Since Worts had walked the same route on the previous evening and the body had not been there, it was fairly easy to establish the time of death to within twenty-four hours. Beale informed the court that he had witnesses who could prove that he was not in Bristol during this critical time.

Next, Mr J.R. Lucas, a surgeon of Long Ashton, gave evidence about the wounds on Charlotte's body, stating that they could have been inflicted by a clasp knife, such as the one later found in Beale's room at Badbey House, Daventry. The knife had what appeared to be a bloodstain on the blade, but, once again, Beale maintained that he had witnesses who could testify that the knife had remained on the pantry shelf in Daventry during his trip to Bristol. Here, the Revd Morehouse intervened, explaining to Beale that the surgeon was not stating that the knife had inflicted the wounds, just that it may have done. Lucas spoke of the difficulty in positively identifying Charlotte's body, which had decomposed rapidly in the hot weather. Although the clothing worn by the dead woman had been identified, Charlotte's body was only positively identified by an abnormality in her teeth, which the surgeon had extracted.

When Inspector Norris of Bath was called to give evidence, he told of finding Charlotte Pugsley's boxes at the prisoner's workplace in Daventry. Beale's only question to Norris was to ask what he intended to do with the money and the watch belonging to him, which had also been seized from Daventry.

Simeon Branscombe, the gardener and gamekeeper who worked at Badbey House, was also called. Beale challenged his evidence, first disputing having said that the luggage belonged to his dead sister, then discussing some bloodstains on the cuffs of a shirt belonging to him, found at Daventry. Branscombe eventually conceded that the blood could have come from a dead rabbit that he had seen Beale carrying shortly before the murder occurred, but refused to be swayed on Beale's explanation of the ownership of the luggage.

Having heard what he described as evidence that was indisputable, Morehouse remanded Beale in custody until the following Friday. He was taken to Taunton Gaol, being returned to Bourton for his next appearance before magistrates. This time, Mr E.M. Harris, a solicitor from Bath, defended Beale. Beale's father and sister (who was very much alive) attended the trial and were granted an interview with the prisoner before he was brought into court.

As soon as the magistrates reconvened, Morehouse announced that they were now satisfied that the blood on Beale's shirt cuffs did not originate from Charlotte Pugsley. Mr Harris then declined the opportunity to cross-examine any of the witnesses from the previous hearing.

Evidence was given regarding the luggage that had been left at the station and Louisa Ford, the housekeeper at Freshford and a great friend of Charlotte, testified to the fact that Charlotte had left with Beale on 9 September. Several witnesses spoke of seeing Beale in Bristol with a woman matching Charlotte's description and one, a Mr Jackson, spoke of seeing the couple walking together in Leigh Woods, he with his arm around her waist and she with her head on his shoulder. William Jones, who worked at the tailor's, told of seeing the small pistol in Beale's coat pocket. Beale said nothing in his own defence and was eventually committed for trial at the next assizes.

The trial was held at Taunton, opening on 22 December 1857 before Mr Justice Willes. Mr Stone and Mr Coleridge appeared for the prosecution, while Harris and T.M. Saunders defended the accused. After hearing much the same evidence as had been presented before the magistrates, the court was told that the case for the prosecution had been constructed so carefully that not a link in the chain of evidence was missing. Counsel for the defence argued that Beale might have been foolish in carrying a loaded pistol, but that foolishness did not make him a murderer. There was nothing to show that Charlotte had not been killed by someone other than Beale. Beale had no motive for killing Charlotte Pugsley and, even if she had met her death by his pistol, it was possible that her death had been accidental.

In summing up the case for the jury, the judge instructed them that Beale could be found either guilty or not guilty of murder – there was nothing in the case that warranted the charge being reduced to one of manslaughter. The jury found the accused man guilty and he was sentenced to hang at Somerset County Gaol.

In the days leading up to his execution, Beale was frequently visited by the prison chaplain and by Revd H.P. Liddon, of Christ Church College Oxford, who was also the vice-principal of the Theological College at Cuddesden. Liddon was the nephew of the prison surgeon and, by chance, knew the prisoner. Despite entreaties from both clergymen to confess and repent his sins, Beale remained tight-lipped to the end. He did make a statement to Liddon in which he intimated that he was not the actual murderer but merely an accessory. However, there was no evidence to support that version of events and since Beale refused to name the man he alleged had committed the killing, he went to the gallows without admitting any culpability in the death of Charlotte Pugsley.

Beale was visited by his wife, his mother and his sisters prior to his execution, which was carried out by William Calcraft on 12 January 1858. A crowd of around 10,000 people assembled at the prison, one fifth of which were women and children. At 9 a.m., the prison bell tolled, signalling that the condemned man had left the prison chapel. Escorted by two warders, Beale walked unhesitatingly to the scaffold where the rope was swiftly placed around his neck and the bolt withdrawn, causing the drop to fall. Beale's body hung for the customary hour before being cut down, later to be buried within the grounds of the gaol.

In May 1858, the reward of 100s offered for the capture of John Beale was divided among several people. Mrs Pickering and Mrs Styles, who had previously worked with Charlotte and had identified her clothing, each received 15s. Ten shillings went to Edwin Aplin, the tailor, and a further 10s to Thomas Jones. Both men had seen and conversed with Beale in Bristol around the time of the murder. The remaining 50s went to Mr Burt, the shoemaker who had recognised the boots that Charlotte wore. The dead woman had, at one time, lodged with Burt and his wife and it was he who had first approached the Bath police with a suggestion as to the identity of the dead woman. Mr Burt had died since the trial and his share of the reward went to his widow.

[Note: In various contemporary accounts, the gamekeeper who discovered Charlotte's body is also referred to as George Worts, George West or George Worth. The name of the house at Daventry is alternatively spelled Badbey and Badby. (Although the first spelling appears most frequently, it is thought that the latter is more likely to be correct since there is a village of Badby near Daventry.) Charlotte's employer is referred to as both Mr Bythsea and the Revd Bythsea, while Mr Burt the shoemaker is also called Mr Bart. Finally, there is some confusion as to the identity of Thomas Jones, who received a proportion of the reward money. It is probable that he is the member of staff at Aplin's the tailors who helped to measure Beale for his suit, although the tailor's assistant's first name is given as William.]

11

'I HAVE NO HOPE AT PRESENT OF MY RECOVERY'

Hotwells, 1868

Fanny Reeves was described in the newspapers of 1869 as having been 'a woman of rather abandoned character' and as 'a very low woman'. By the time she was in her early twenties, she had given birth to an illegitimate child. She was also an habitual drunkard and was known to be violent.

Somehow Fanny crossed paths with Henry Jenkins, a respectable married man who worked as a ship's carpenter and was described as quiet and inoffensive. The result of their association was a second illegitimate child for Fanny and a parish order for Henry to maintain the child by paying Fanny the sum of 2s each week.

By October 1868, Henry was in arrears with his payments by £1 7s and Fanny was furious. Accordingly, on 16 October, she arranged to meet Henry at the Cumberland Docks and, as soon as he arrived, she angrily demanded money from him. Henry tried to placate her, telling her that he did not have any money but, if she would walk with him, then he would try to get some.

The couple walked to Cumberland Terrace in Hotwells and Henry went into a house, returning a few minutes later with the news that he had been unable to get any money. Predictably, Fanny was livid and, as the couple continued to walk up the road, more angry words were exchanged between them.

When they reached the River Avon, Henry suddenly stopped and pointed at the water. 'Here's a rat climbing up the river bank' he said and, as Fanny leaned forward to try and see it, he shouted 'Take that!' and pushed her hard with both hands, sending her flying into the water.

Fanny managed to cling onto the riverbank and the sound of the splash as she entered the water, followed by her frantic screams, brought a nearby policeman rushing to her aid. She was dragged from the river wet, cold and exhausted and taken to her mother's house and put to bed.

Cumberland Basin and Hotwells, 1920s. (Author's collection)

By the following day, Fanny was still weak and debilitated and a doctor was sent for at around midday. Fanny expressed a belief that she was going to die so a minister was also called, spending some time praying with her at her bedside. The doctor made a second visit that evening and found Fanny's condition to have worsened. By now, her heartbeat was racing and her breathing was so laboured that it was thought prudent to summon a magistrate to record her deposition.

After swearing an oath, she dictated her statement, which was faithfully recorded by the magistrate's clerk and, having done so, was asked by the magistrate if she had made her statement without hope of recovery. 'None', was her reply. 'I have no hope of my recovery', wrote the clerk. The magistrate then read the statement out to her, asking her to correct any mistakes she might have made. When he had finished reading, Fanny suggested the addition of the words 'at present'. The clerk amended the statement accordingly and it was once again read out to her. Now, the statement read, 'I have no hope at present of my recovery'. Fanny was then satisfied that the deposition was accurate and signed it with her mark. She died the following morning at around 11 a.m.

The same surgeon who had attended her before her death conducted the post-mortem examination, assisted by one of his colleagues. They found that Fanny had been extremely healthy, the only damage to her organs being congestion of both lungs. The surgeons noted that there was evidence of long-standing lung disease but attributed the cause of her death to congestion of the lungs brought on by sudden cold and immersion in the river.

Henry Jenkins was promptly arrested, not without some difficulty since he persistently denied that he was Henry Jenkins. When he could deny his identity no longer, he then denied having pushed Fanny, maintaining that she must have stumbled and fallen into the river while intoxicated.

Jenkins stood trial for the wilful murder of Fanny Reeves at the Bristol Assizes. The proceedings opened on 3 April 1869 before Mr Justice Byles, with Mr T.W. Saunders and Mr Bailey prosecuting and Mr Collins and Mr Norris acting for the defence. Immediately after the trial began, Collins tried to have it halted on the grounds that a 'most material witness' for the prisoner had not yet arrived. On learning that the witness lived in Newport, the judge suggested that a telegraph be sent asking him to attend and said that, if he came by train, there was a good possibility that he would arrive before he was actually needed. Collins protested that he feared the witness was coming by water and might be prevented from landing because of the low tide on the river. 'We must do the best we can', replied the judge and insisted that the trial continue.

As the trial progressed, it became apparent that there was no real evidence against Henry Jenkins apart from the dying declaration of Fanny Reeves, and the legality of that declaration was about to be questioned.

Cleverly, Collins objected to the inclusion of the deposition as evidence against his client. In order for the declaration to be admissible, it had to have been made under the impression of impending death. Any hope of recovery would make the declaration invalid and, by insisting on the insertion of the words 'at present', Miss Reeves had clearly demonstrated that all hope was not excluded.

Saunders refuted his objections, saying that on the contrary; by expressing a wish for someone to be sent for to pray over her and saying that she did not think she would get over this, Fanny had clearly demonstrated that she expected to die. Although she was in poor physical condition at the time of her statement, Fanny was completely clear in her mind and her belief was that she was past recovery.

Forced to rule on the matter, the judge said that, since the entire case depended on the admissibility of this statement, then he felt he should admit it. However, he did indicate to the jury that they should consider the objection as a point in favour of the defendant.

The court heard from the medical witnesses and the magistrate's clerk who had recorded Fanny Reeves's deposition. It was then left for Mr Collins to address the jury in defence of his client.

Collins pointed out that the whole case depended on the testimony of Fanny Reeves and that, of course, he was unable to cross-examine her since she was dead. It was, he said, most difficult to attack the character or truthfulness of one who was dead, but it was his job to secure justice for the living. It pained him to be unable to spare Fanny's character but he asked the jury to consider what kind of woman Fanny really was.

There was no dispute that, some years ago, she and the prisoner were 'connected' (a contemporary euphemism for being sexually active). However, since then, Fanny had become a slovenly, drunken, dissipated woman who behaved more like a mad woman when drunk than one who was sane. She had threatened to commit suicide on numerous occasions, usually saying that she would drown herself.

Jenkins, on the other hand, was a sober, steady, hard-working man of excellent character on which there was not the slightest stain or blot.

Collins then attacked the admissibility of the deposition once more and went on to call numerous witnesses to attest to the fine, upstanding character of his client before finally calling a surprise witness – Henry Jenkins's father.

Mr Jenkins Senior testified that his son was at home at the time that he heard that a woman had fallen into the water – he himself had gone to his son's house to tell him about the incident as soon as it had happened and found his son there, busy repairing a table. Mr Jenkins's evidence was corroborated by his daughter, Henry's sister. If these witnesses were to be believed, Collins told the jury, then Henry Jenkins had an alibi for the murder of Fanny Reeves. He could not have killed her.

Having listened to the judge's summary of the case, the jury retired, returning with a verdict of 'Guilty'. Jenkins was sentenced to death and taken from the court to await his fate.

He was kept in the prison infirmary while preparations were made for his execution by erecting a gallows on the prison lawn. However, Collins was like a terrier with a bone in defence of his client and was not about to let the matter rest.

He appealed the conviction, citing the two words 'at present' in Fanny's deposition as evidence that all hope of her recovery had not yet died. Collins succeeded in getting a hearing in the Court of Criminal Appeal, where the matter was discussed before Lord Chief Baron Kelly, Baron Cleasby and Justices Byles, Lush and Brett.

Collins cited a number of cases in which it had previously been ruled that 'there must be a settled, hopeless expectation of death in the person making the declaration and that all hope must be excluded.' By insisting on the insertion of the words 'at present' argued Collins, Fanny had not excluded all hope.

Their Lordships agreed unanimously that the insertion of the two words made the statement of the dead woman inadmissible as evidence and, since that statement was the only evidence against the prisoner, they had no option but to quash his conviction.

When told of the decision, Jenkins, who had quietly but steadfastly maintained his innocence, had just four words to say; 'Thank God for that!' He was released as soon as the official order from the Court of Appeal arrived at the prison, having spent just over six months living under the shadow of the hangman's noose.

12

'HOW DIDST COME TO SWEAR FALSE?'

St George, 1869

Harriet Nurse was a 36-year-old widow who earned her living selling fish, fruit and vegetables. On Saturday 30 January 1869, after a long day working at Bristol market, she called into the Pied Horse public house where she enjoyed several glasses of cider before moving on to the Air Balloon. By 10.15 p.m., Mrs Nurse was described as being quite drunk and 'thick of utterance'.

It was a windy night, very dark and raining heavily when Harriet finally staggered out of the pub to make her way home. The son of the landlord escorted her for the first 30yds of her journey but, even in this short distance, she fell over twice.

Two more customers left the Air Balloon at about 10.40 p.m. and found Harriet lying in the road. They dragged her to her feet and walked with her for a further 200yds, at which point she tugged on the arm of Mr Bennett, one of her helpers, indicating that they should turn off to the right. Bennett led her along the right-hand path to a gate, where he left her before retracing his steps back to his own road home.

At around midnight, a Mr Kenney was travelling home from Bristol. As he walked along Rose and Crown Lane in the pitch dark, he thought he saw a body lying on a grassy bank at the roadside. Kenney went straight to the nearest house, where he roused the occupant, an old man named Mr Hope. Somewhat reluctantly, Hope lit a candle and walked back with Mr Kenney in search of the body. However, the wind soon blew the candle out, at which point Mr Hope began to suspect that Kenny was playing a practical joke on him and returned home. In foul weather and with no light, Kenney too decided to abandon the search and continue home.

At 7 a.m. on the following morning, a Mr Golding was walking along the lane leading to the Air Balloon pub and, at the corner where it joined Rose and Crown Lane, his attention was drawn to a hayrick, which was surrounded by a fence made of chain. There was a gate in the fence, which was topped with thorns, and caught in the thorns and fluttering in the breeze was a torn pair of women's 'drawers'.

The Pied Horse, 2007. (©R. Sly)

The Air Balloon Tavern, 2007. (©R. Sly)

As Golding approached the hayrick for a closer look, he noticed the body of a woman lying about 20yds inside the chain fence. The woman lay on her back, her eyes open and staring. Her skirts were pulled up exposing her genitals and her bodice was undone. One hand was clutched to her bare breasts.

The police were called and the first officer to arrive, Sergeant Bird, ordered the woman's body to be removed to a stable at the nearby Rose and Crown public house. A surgeon, Dr Grace, examined the body and quickly put paid to Bird's first theory, which was that the woman had been raped and then murdered. In Dr Grace's opinion, the dead woman's injuries were more consistent with her having hurt herself climbing over the thorn-topped gate.

Sergeant Bird disagreed. He had noticed that the woman had marks around her mouth that he suspected had been caused by fingernails and that there were also bruises on her wrists that looked as though they may have been the result of her being restrained by holding her arms very firmly. A local woman who washed the woman's body also saw these marks, but, on a second examination of the body on the following day, Dr Grace and another surgeon still failed to notice them.

Dr Grace did note that the deceased had bruises on her knees and elbows and a small scratch on her forehead. The crevices in her face and ears were filled with mud, and dirt was found packed between her teeth and the inside of her cheek. Her hair was matted with mud and a single dog-rose berry, identical to those in the thorns on the gate, was found in her stays. The dead woman had recently been intimate with a man, but Dr Grace did not believe that she had been violated. In his opinion, the cause of the woman's death had either been due to exposure to the elements on the cold, rainy night, or suffocation.

Mr Lodge, a surgeon who made yet another post-mortem examination on the woman five days after the discovery of her body, could not agree with Dr Grace's opinions. Like Sergeant Bird, he too observed the marks around the woman's mouth and determined her death to have been caused by suffocation, either by pressure from a man's hand or by the woman having had her face forced down into the mud, preventing her from breathing.

By now, the dead woman had been identified as Harriet Nurse and the police were soon to receive some very interesting information about her murder from a man named Milsom.

On the night of Mrs Nurse's death, Milsom had been drinking in the Rose and Crown pub, which stood at the end of the lane in which Harriet's body had been found. His drinking companion that evening had been a man named Charles Wiltshire and, when the public house had closed at around midnight, Milsom and Wiltshire had lingered outside in the road, talking for some time. According to Milsom, Wiltshire had been trying to persuade him to steal some chickens, but Milsom had refused.

Eventually, the two men set off to walk down Rose and Crown Lane. As they walked, they spotted the dark shape of another person in front of them and Wiltshire told Milsom that he hoped that it was a woman as, if it were, he would have what the newspapers of the day referred to as 'criminal intimacy' with her.

The person was indeed a woman – it was Harriet Nurse, sitting partially reclined on the bank, supporting herself on her elbows. Milsom told the police that Wiltshire had pulled off the woman's shawl and thrown it over the hedge.

He had then laid down on top of the woman, at which she had cried out two or three times.

Wiltshire had rubbed mud into her face and had tried to persuade Milsom to hold his hand over her mouth to quieten her, but Milsom had refused. He had twice pulled Wiltshire off the woman, but Wiltshire had brushed him aside and continued with his attempts to have intercourse with Harriet. Milsom, a much smaller man, realised that he was not going to be able to prevent Wiltshire's assault on the woman and had eventually walked away, leaving Harriet to her fate.

Wiltshire had caught him up a few minutes later and told him that the woman was one of the Kellys – a name by which Harriet Nurse was also known. Together, the two men had gone to the house of Wiltshire's brother, Aaron, where Milsom spoke about the night's events. Aaron had not been at all surprised, saying that Charles was liable to do such things when he was drunk.

While Milsom stayed at the house, Wiltshire subsequently left and was absent for some time. When he returned, the two went on to the house of a friend, Mr Haden. Again, Wiltshire left the house for some time alone, while Milsom stayed behind.

Following Milsom's statement to the police, Charles Wiltshire was interviewed and, not surprisingly, gave a completely different account of events. He freely admitted to being with Milsom on the night of the murder, but swore that he had neither touched nor hurt Harriet Nurse. His only contact with the deceased occurred when Milsom had pushed him down onto her.

Wiltshire's house was searched on 5 February and the coat that he had been wearing on the night of the murder was seized. It was still wet, either from the pouring rain or because it had been cleaned and it had what looked like patches of blood on the left sleeve. Wiltshire's boots were also found hidden under the floorboards and it was noted that they bore traces of hay burrs. The finding of the clothes, coupled with Milsom's statement, was judged to be sufficient evidence against Wiltshire for him to be arrested and charged with the wilful murder of Harriet Nurse.

Wiltshire was tried at Gloucester Crown Court on 3 April 1869 before Mr Justice Hannen. Mr Sawyer and Mr George Griffiths handled the prosecution while Mr J.O. Griffiths (no relation) defended the accused.

From the outset, Wiltshire's defence counsel attacked Milsom's statement, pointing out that Milsom was at very least an accomplice to the murder and, if he were to change places with Wiltshire in the dock, then the evidence against him would be just as strong. In addition, Mr J.O. Griffiths pointed out the differing opinions of the doctors who had examined Mrs Nurse after her death. While it was agreed that she had had sexual intercourse before she died, it was impossible to determine whether or not this was consensual and, even if she had been raped, there was nothing whatsoever to suggest that it was his client who had raped her.

Griffiths pointed out that Harriet had been in a state of extreme drunkenness when she died and it was entirely possible that she had simply passed out, either falling face down in the mud and suffocating or succumbing to the cold, rainy night and dying of exposure.

In his summing up of the case, Mr Justice Hannen said that he would leave it up to the jury to decide whether or not they believed that Mrs Nurse had died as a consequence of the actions of Charles Wiltshire. He pointed out that some of the findings corroborated Milsom's statement. The dead woman's shawl had subsequently been found exactly where Milsom maintained it had been thrown and the dirt on the dead woman's face was consistent with her having had mud rubbed into it, something that Milsom had sworn under oath that he had seen Wiltshire do.

The judge then clarified the law for the jury. If they believed that the accused had, in the course of his violation of the victim, pressed his hand over her mouth to silence her and suffocated her in doing so, then their verdict must be guilty of murder. The verdict would be the same if the effect of the rape had been such that it had rendered the victim incapable of resisting the cold, wet weather, causing her to die of exposure. If, however, the jury believed that the victim, in her drunken condition, would have died of exposure anyway, even if there had been no violation, then they must find the prisoner not guilty.

The jury deliberated for about twenty minutes before returning with their verdict, finding Charles Wiltshire guilty of the wilful murder of Harriet Nurse. Not without emotion, the judge passed sentence of death.

The defence counsel immediately announced his intention to appeal the sentence. Wiltshire's account of events on the night of the murder had differed from Milsom's and Mr J.O. Griffiths strongly felt that there was sufficient doubt as to which of the two men had committed the crime to justify clemency for his client.

Wiltshire freely admitted to being in the Rose and Crown public house with Milsom on the night of the murder and to agreeing to go and steal some chickens. However, he maintained that when they had stumbled upon Harriet Nurse lying on the side of the lane, it had been Milsom who had first raped her and then incited him to do the same. When Milsom had finished with the woman, he had picked up her shawl and thrown it over the hedge.

The two men had then left the woman and continued on their way to the home of Aaron Wiltshire. When they were nearly there, Milsom had suddenly stopped and asked Wiltshire if he thought that Nurse might have had any money on her.

The two men had retraced their steps and, on reaching Harriet Nurse, had begun to search her. As soon as they touched her, Harriet had come to her senses and began to scream 'Murder!' at the top of her voice.

This had angered Milsom, who had smacked her hard across the mouth and then ripped off her underclothes and threw them over the hedge, digging his fingers into the bodice of her dress and ripping it apart. At this stage, Milsom's dog had also grabbed hold of Harriet and had consequently been given a kicking by his master.

According to Wiltshire, Milsom had then exhibited some 'most indecent conduct and language', but was interrupted in his second rape of the victim by what the two men thought was the sound of approaching footsteps.

They had escaped to the safety of Wiltshire's brother's home, where they had related the night's events to Aaron Wiltshire. From there, they had followed their original plan of stealing a chicken, but had been disturbed by the farmer and had run away in opposite directions.

Wiltshire then admitted to returning to the scene of the crime alone. Remembering that there had been a hayrick near to where they had left

Mrs Nurse, he decided to steal some hay for his donkey. Still clutching the chicken he had stolen, as he approached the hayrick, he heard her still calling out 'Murder!' He described going to check on her and finding her lying half across the thorn-topped gate, her upper body hanging down on one side with her skirts over her head. One of her shoes was held fast by thorns.

Wiltshire had freed the woman's shoe, which she had pitched headfirst over the gate. He had then left her, apparently still alive and crying 'Murder!' and returned to his home.

On the following morning, he had received a visit from Isaac and Aaron, his two brothers. Isaac, knowing nothing of the events of the early hours of the morning, broke the news of the discovery of the dead body to Charles and his wife, to which Charles had responded, 'That's a bad job.' A few minutes later, Charles and Aaron had had a chance to talk privately and both agreed to say nothing to anyone in order to protect Milsom. They obviously did not expect Milsom to be the one to do the talking.

Wiltshire and Milsom met in Lawford's Gate Prison, when Wiltshire had asked Milsom, 'How didst come to swear false?' Milsom explained that he had been incited to do so by two other people, then said that he would say whatever was necessary to clear his name and suggested that Wiltshire do the same.

The Court of Appeal agreed that there was insufficient evidence to find Charles Wiltshire guilty of murder and his sentence was commuted to life imprisonment. On hearing the news, Wilthire announced that he was thankful to God for sparing his life but sorry that he would be parted from his wife for the rest of his days. He put his trouble down to the fact that he had deserted his religious upbringing and urged others to be sure to follow the ways of the Lord.

There does not seem to be any record of Milsom standing trial for his part in the rape and murder of Harriet Nurse.

13

'CAN YOU PROVE IT?'

St Philips, 1869

At about 9 o'clock on the morning of 24 April 1869, William Thomas Curtis, a baker from West Street, heard a commotion coming from nearby Waterloo Street. When he went to see what all the noise was about, he found a donkey pulling a cart. Two young men were beating the poor beast, ill-treating it so cruelly that Curtis felt obliged to remonstrate with the pair, both on their abuse of the animal and on their use of filthy language in front of a number of women. His intervention earned him a tirade of swearing, at which Curtis beat a hasty retreat back to his shop.

The two young men followed him. While one remained outside, the other entered the shop where he continued to use bad language. Curtis told him in no uncertain terms that if he didn't leave the shop immediately, then he would be kicked out. The young man left, but only went as far as the pavement outside, from where he continued to hurl insults and obscenities at the baker.

Curtis went to the shop door and threatened the young man that, if he didn't go away, he would be arrested. The swearing continued unabated, so Curtis left in search of a police officer, closely followed by the loud and abusive youth.

They had not gone far when the verbal threats escalated to physical ones. The young man – later identified as 19-year-old William Pullin – jumped Curtis and began to hit him about the face and head.

At that point, a passer-by intervened. Richard Hill, aged 31, was in fact PC 273, a Bristol police constable and although he was on duty, he was not in uniform that day. Hill tried to take charge of the situation. Telling Curtis to stand aside, he said that he had seen quite enough and, taking Pullin by the collar, announced his intention of taking him into custody.

At that, Pullin turned, wriggled free from Hill's grasp and bolted into a nearby pub, closely followed by a large crowd of onlookers, all of whom, it seemed, had more sympathy for Pullin than for the man trying to apprehend him. As Hill grappled to arrest Pullin, the young man grabbed hold of the bar counter and clung on for grim death.

Curtis stepped forward to assist PC Hill and between them, they managed to prise Pullin's fingers free. However, in the ensuing melee, all three men fell to the ground, with Pullin underneath, and Curtis received a kick in the head that rendered him senseless. Meanwhile, a witness, George Cole, had run to St Philips police station for reinforcements and two constables were immediately despatched to Hill's aid. By the time they arrived, what had originally been a struggle between Hill and Pullin had fast become a large-scale fight and yet more police officers were sent into the fray. Finally Pullin was overpowered and escorted to the police station at St Philips, fighting all the way.

Only then was it noticed that there was a large pool of blood on the floor of the pub and that PC Hill was very pale. He made his way shakily over to the bar of the pub where he told the landlady, 'Mrs Osborne, I've been stabbed.' Hill was given a tot of brandy and taken to a quiet back room, where he quickly lapsed into unconsciousness. A surgeon, Mr T.H.W. Davies, was summoned but, as soon as he saw PC Hill, he realised that the situation was hopeless and that there was nothing he could do to save the injured man's life. Hill died a few minutes later. He was due to have been married that very week.

At the police station, Pullin was charged with 'wilfully and feloniously killing and slaying PC 273 in the lawful execution of his duty.' Pullen accepted the charge indifferently, his only comment being, 'Can you prove it?'

At a post-mortem examination, PC Hill was found to have two stab wounds, one above and one below his left knee. The one below the knee was superficial, but the one above the knee had penetrated to a depth of 2in, cutting an artery and causing Hill to bleed to death fairly rapidly.

The area of Bristol in which Hill met his death was, in those days, a violent place, where even in broad daylight police officers traditionally patrolled in pairs or threes. Described in a newspaper of the time as 'a place of unsavoury repute, notorious as a den of tramps and one of the worst districts in the east end of the city', so reviled were the police that it was said that any lone officer risked being thrown into the river. Yet, when PC Hill was buried, tens of thousands of people silently lined the streets to pay their last respects as his cortège passed on its way to Arnos Vale Cemetery. His plain coffin was followed by his fiancée, then by 160 of his fellow officers, marching in ranks of four.

Pullin's trial opened before Mr Justice Keating in mid-August 1869. Mr Saunders and Mr Bailey conducted the prosecution, while Mr Collins and Mr Norris defended Pullin, who pleaded 'Not Guilty'.

One of the first witnesses to be called was Curtis, the baker. He stated in the witness box that he had initially been unaware that Hill was a police officer and that he could not say whether Pullin went into the Three Horse Shoes pub on Gloucester Lane of his own volition, or whether he was simply propelled there by the large, hostile crowd that had gathered to watch the incident. Curtis described Pullin as having been 'very tipsy'.

Another witness, who knew both Hill and Pullin, described Pullin as more drunk than she had ever seen him before – like a madman. She had admonished him; 'Bill, you had better go quietly with that man, as you will have to go.' Her advice had not been heeded.

Several witnesses attested to seeing Pullin with a knife in his hand and to hearing him threaten to stab PC Hill if he didn't let go of him. Pullin was so drunk and enraged, that it had taken four officers to get him to the police station and a large, bloodstained clasp knife had subsequently been found on their route in the early hours of the morning after the stabbing. It was thought that, in all the confusion, Pullin had somehow managed to throw away his knife in Braggs Lane without the escorting officers noticing.

Mr Collins, for the defence, outlined three options for the jury. They could, he argued, find his client guilty of murder, guilty of manslaughter, or they could find him not guilty and acquit him. He asked the jury what evidence there was to suggest that Pullin committed the stabbing with malice aforethought. His client was in a state of mad intoxication at the time and there was nothing about Hill that suggested that he was a police officer. Surely, maintained Collins, if his client had intended to kill Hill, he would have stabbed him in a more vital part than his knee. Collins raised other anomalies about the evidence. How could Pullin have dropped the knife on the way to the police station without it being noticed by one of the officers escorting him? Were the jury fully satisfied that Pullin actually had a knife at all? Given that he was clinging desperately to the bar and also a 'beer engine handle' in an effort to prevent himself being dragged to the police station, when did he have his hands free for long enough to remove a knife from his pocket? Was it not possible that another member of the large, unruly crowd might have stabbed the constable?

Mr Justice Keating then summed up the facts of the case for the jury. He asked them if the deceased was, at the time of the stabbing, engaged in the execution of his duty? Did the prisoner actually inflict the fatal wound? If a man with a weapon inflicted a wound intentionally, then the law would presume malice and, if a constable on duty was resisted, then such resistance was unlawful. If this unlawful resistance ultimately caused the death of the constable, then the only possible verdict was guilty of murder. If, on the other hand, the jury were not satisfied that the defendant knew that Hill was a police officer, even if he inflicted the wound intentionally, then the proper verdict would be manslaughter.

The jury retired for two hours before returning a verdict of guilty of murder of a police constable while infuriated by drink. The judge donned his traditional black cap, ignoring the jury's recommendations that Pullin should not face the death penalty on account of his youth and his previous good character. Pullin wept bitterly as the death sentence was pronounced.

But Keating had reckoned without public opinion. More than 7,000 people signed a petition for clemency and Pullin's death sentence was eventually commuted to life imprisonment.

Richard Hill, a courageous man who, even at great risk to his own personal safety, was not prepared to let an injustice go unpunished, is commemorated by a marble tablet, currently located in the foyer of the police station at Trinity Road. The tablet, paid for by donation from his fellow officers and by inhabitants of the city, is inscribed with the words:

In memory of Richard Hill, police constable of this city, who was murdered while in the execution of his duty in Gloucester Lane, 24 April 1869, aged 31 years, and was interred in Arnos Vale Cemetery.

[Note: In various contemporary accounts of the murder of PC Hill, his killer's name is alternatively spelled Pullen.]

14

'THIS IS JUST WHAT MY DREAM TOLD ME I WOULD COME TO'

Horfield, 1873

Edwin Bailey had a better start in life than could be expected for most illegitimate babies in Victorian England. He was born in Winterbourne, Gloucestershire, then the centre of the hat making industry, to parents who both worked in the trade. Edwin was brought up in his grandparents' home, attending the Winterbourne National School until, at 16 years of age, he was apprenticed to a boot maker in Downend.

His apprenticeship lasted less than a week. He was sent home in disgrace after his employer's wife made a serious complaint against him, which one can only assume was of a sexual nature. His history for the next few years is not known but by 1860 he was working in a shoe shop in Mary-Le-Port Street. His uncle later bought the business and promoted him to manager but before long the two quarrelled and Edwin found himself unemployed.

Having no money or job, Edwin then married his landlady who was comparatively wealthy. Using her money, he and a friend went into the wholesale business together but the business failed, forcing Edwin into bankruptcy. His friend lost literally everything he owned in the disastrous venture and died shortly afterwards.

When a building on St Augustine's Parade leased to Edwin mysteriously caught fire, it was believed that the fire was not accidental. Unfortunately for Edwin, the blaze was extinguished before it could do much damage, thus wrecking his hopes of a substantial insurance claim. Edwin made himself scarce and travelled to London, where he worked in a tavern for a year before returning to his wife in Bristol. However, once again, he didn't stay in Bristol long and was soon working in a boot shop in Gloucestershire where, conveniently forgetting about his long-suffering wife, he began to court one of the other assistants at the shop. He picked the wrong girl to trifle with. Her father was a policeman and when he

Clifton from Ashton Meadows. (Author's collection)

was informed about Edwin's marital status, he had him run out of town to save his daughter's honour. Back in Bristol once more, Edwin set up a boot shop of his own in Clifton, financed, of course, by his wife.

In 1871, a young maid, Mary Jenkins, was sent to Edwin's shop to have some boots repaired. Edwin allegedly seized the young girl and dragged her into the back of the shop where he gagged and raped her. A complaint was made to the police, but somehow Edwin managed to avoid any serious consequences and, in 1872, he assaulted the same young woman again, this time impregnating her.

Mary Jenkins gave birth to a daughter, Sarah, on 23 October 1872 and, although Edwin denied that he was the child's father, he was unable to convince the local magistrates who ordered him to support the child by paying a weekly sum of *5s* until her sixteenth birthday. It appeared that Edwin was, at the time, also paying child support for another illegitimate baby, whose mother lived in Easton.

Mary and her baby were welcomed into her parents' home in Horfield and, when Mary found another job, her mother Elizabeth agreed to look after the child while she worked.

It was at about this time that a woman named Anne Barry inveigled herself into the Jenkins household. She told the family that little Sarah reminded her of her own baby, which had sadly died, and she was soon making regular visits. Barry mentioned a charitable society to the family, telling them that she had given their name to the 'Dorcas Society' and that someone would be writing to them within a few days.

Sure enough, a letter arrived from a Jane Isabella Smith of Hope Cottages, Cotham. In it were enclosed some Steedman's Soothing Powders for baby Sarah, who had been suffering badly from teething pains and colic. When Anne Barry next visited, she was told about the powders and recommended them highly to the family in preference to the magnesium mixture they had been using previously.

She also told them that she was moving to a distant part of Bristol and so would not be visiting again.

Mary and Elizabeth Jenkins wrote a thank-you letter to Jane Smith and, on her next day off on 17 August 1873, Mary gave baby Sarah some of the powders to ease her red, swollen gums.

Within seconds, the baby began to scream and would not be comforted. Soon, baby Sarah began to stiffen and her little face turned first red, then black. Mary at once ran for a doctor but by the time she returned, Sarah had died. On analysis, the teething powders were found to contain a strychnine-based rat poison.

Naturally, the first task for the police was to trace the source of the Steedman's Powders. But when they went in search of Isabella Jane Smith, they found that she didn't exist and the thank-you letter that Mary and her mother had written had ended up in the Post Office's dead letter department.

Next, the police interviewed Edwin Bailey at his shop and found samples of writing paper and envelopes exactly matching those used for the letter that purported to come from Miss Smith. Several months previously, Bailey had been heard to have offered half a sovereign to anyone who could bring him news of the baby's death – hence he was arrested. So was Anne Barry, who turned out to be the charlady who cleaned Edwin's shop to supplement her income as a back street midwife. Bailey was charged with wilful murder, while Barry was charged with aiding and abetting.

Barry swore that she was innocent of anything other than trying to find out who had fathered baby Sarah, since Bailey was convinced that the child was not his. Whether Bailey had paid her to do this, or whether she was simply infatuated with him is not clear, although she professed to be very much in love with her husband. Bailey also denied any involvement in the death of Sarah and continued to deny paternity.

Bailey and Barry were brought before magistrates at Lawford's Gate Court and committed for trial before Judge Archibald. Both were found guilty and although the jury put forward a recommendation for mercy, both were sentenced to death. Despite numerous petitions for the commutation of their sentences, they faced the hangman at Gloucester Prison on 12 January 1874 in the company of Charles Edward Butt, who had shot a young woman at Arlingham. By coincidence, both murders had taken place on the same day.

Both Bailey and Barry made a full confession shortly before their executions, although 32-year-old Edwin insisted to the end that he had not fathered Sarah. His wife and family visited him in prison during his last few days – and he also wrote a farewell letter and a poem to a 'Miss M', possibly the woman from Easton with whom he was alleged to have another illegitimate daughter.

The hangman was expected to be William Calcraft. However, the veteran executioner was at that time 78 years old and unwell. His assistant, Robert Anderson, carried out the three executions and afterwards admitted that he had only brought enough rope for two, since he had expected Barry to be acquitted.

Anne, aged 31, went to her death dressed in a pale print gown and whispered to the hangman as he adjusted the noose around her neck, 'This is just what my dream told me I would come to.' Of the three prisoners, it was Anne who took the longest to die – her slight build meant that, after almost three minutes, the executioner had to press down on her body in order to complete his task.

15

'THIS IS ALL THROUGH A DRUNKEN WIFE'

Temple, 1874

By 1874, William and Alice Hole had been married for thirty years. The marriage had once been a happy one, but it soured very rapidly after tragedy struck the couple, when their only son was killed.

Hole, who was then the landlord of the Castle of Comfort tavern in Tower Street, Temple, took his bereavement particularly badly. He sank into a deep depression and eventually tried unsuccessfully to drown himself. Then, three years later, he suffered a serious accident when he fell from a horse-drawn gig as it travelled through St George.

Having sustained head injuries in the accident, he was carried, unconscious, to a nearby public house. It took a full hour before he came to his senses again, but the accident left him prone to terrible incapacitating headaches, which plagued him for the rest of his life.

Hole eventually gave up the tenancy of his pub and set about building a successful barge business. By 1849, the barge owner employed several men and was carrying out regular contract work for the local railways. Yet, in spite of his success, both his mental and physical health were still poor.

Still suffering from serious headaches and crippling bouts of black depression, William made regular threats of suicide and on one occasion, his maidservant, Sarah Crocombe, had to wrestle a knife from him after he determined to 'do away with himself'. William began to hear voices and to suffer from bouts of paranoia and delusions and took to wandering about in the middle of the night, often leaving the house and disappearing for several hours. Formerly a teetotaller, he began to drink heavily and, before long, was very rarely sober. Alice also eventually took to drink and the more alcohol the couple drank, the more frequent and violent their arguments became.

Tower Street, 2007. (©N. Sly)

On 28 August, 52-year-old William had been complaining all day of a bad headache and, by early evening, he had turned to alcohol to blot out the pain. Sarah Crocombe had enjoyed an evening off and, when she returned home shortly after 10.30 p.m., it was to find Alice outside the house, slumped on the doorstep in a state of intoxication. Sarah tried to persuade her mistress to come inside but Alice refused, so Sarah went indoors alone and made herself some supper. Shortly afterwards, she popped out again for a brief visit with her brother who lived nearby. She paused to chat to a neighbour on her way back, but the conversation was suddenly interrupted by loud screams of 'Murder!'

While Sarah had been away, Henrietta Dodge had stepped outside to stand by her front door for a breath of fresh air. She had seen Alice sitting on the doorstep and watched as William came staggering down the street towards her.

As soon as Alice spotted William, she beat a hasty retreat into the house but emerged a few minutes later, shouting, 'You old blackguard!' William followed close behind her. He swung a punch at his wife, knocking her to the ground, then turned on his heel and went back inside, locking the door behind him. Alice reeled drunkenly to another neighbour's doorstep and sat there pitifully for a few minutes before returning once more to her own doorstep. At that point, she spotted Henrietta and approached her unsteadily. 'I shan't go in tonight', she told Mrs Dodge, who promptly pointed out that she would be obliged to if the police came around.

Then the door to Alice's house opened and William appeared framed in the doorway. He asked Alice to come in, but when she refused, he slammed the door violently shut. Shortly afterwards he reappeared and angrily repeated his request.

'When I like', said Alice defiantly, at which her husband strode out into the street, hit her again, then immediately went back indoors. Moments later he was back out in the street, this time brandishing a carving knife with an 8in blade.

As Henrietta Dodge watched in horror, William lunged at his wife, sending her sprawling to the ground. He then bent over her and made two quick slashes with the carving knife across Alice's throat.

Terrified, Henrietta Dodge ran back into her own house, fumbling desperately to bolt the door behind her. She could hear Alice Hole calling her name and shouting 'Murder!' and eventually opened her front door slightly and peered through the crack.

Illuminated by a nearby streetlamp was a ghastly scene. Alice Hole was slumped against the kerb, her arms waving, with blood pumping from her throat. William had once again retreated to his own house and was sitting calmly on his windowsill. Henrietta immediately went into hysterics, but fortunately by that time, more neighbours had arrived on the scene.

Jane Morrish and Mary Cotterell rushed to the aid of the stricken woman, Mary kneeling to comfort her, while Jane hurried to the nearby pub to get towels to try and stem the flow of blood. Two more neighbours, George Perry and Samuel Milsom, apprehended William, with Milsom taking charge of the knife. Someone else ran to fetch a doctor and summon the police.

Jane and Mary asked William to help them carry Alice into the house but he refused, saying, 'She shan't come in. Take her anywhere; I have killed her and I shall be hung.' With difficulty, the two women managed between them to carry Alice into her house and lay her on the living room rug. She was bleeding profusely and unfortunately, the arterial blood loss was so great that she died before the arrival of the doctor. When told that his wife was dead, William shook his head sorrowfully and said, 'Brandy. Brandy has done it.'

William begged Milsom to return his knife but, fearing that he may use it on himself, Milsom refused. By the time the first policeman arrived, Hole seemed resigned to his fate, telling the officer, 'Here I am. I did it. I shall not run away. Take me if you like.'

As the officer made to arrest him, Hole asked if he might have one last brandy and water, since it would be a long while before he had the chance to drink one again. His request was refused and he was escorted to Bedminster police station, where he was formally charged with the murder of his wife.

'This is all through a drunken wife', he told the police and, despite being warned by the officers not to incriminate himself, he insisted on confessing to the killing and giving the officers a demonstration in mime as to how he had actually committed the murder. He then begged to be allowed to drown himself and tried to strangle himself with his silk handkerchief. Deprived of alcohol once in prison, he soon began to suffer from delirium tremens and seizures.

His trial opened at the Bristol Assizes on 3 April 1875, with Mr Norris and Mr Matthews acting for the prosecution and Mr Collins and Mr Cotton defending. The defence pleaded insanity on the grounds of Hole's alcoholism and the head injuries he had received in his accident – plus the fact that he had been indisputably blind drunk at the time of the murder. However, the judge told the jury in his summary of the case that if Hole knew that the nature of the act

Bedminster police station. (Courtesy of Derek Fisher, Bygone Bristol)

he had committed was wrong, then he was to be held responsible for his wife's murder.

Given that Hole had admitted responsibility for his actions immediately after attacking his wife, telling the two neighbours that he would be hung, it was impossible to believe that he did not understand the act or the probable consequences of his actions. Accordingly, after a short deliberation, the jury returned a verdict of 'Guilty' and Hole was sentenced to death. On receiving his sentence, he responded, 'I know nothing about it. I shall die happy.'

While Hole languished in Bristol Prison, seemingly indifferent to his fate, strenuous efforts were made on his behalf to try and obtain a reprieve on the grounds that he had been insensible with drink at the time of the offence and therefore was not accountable for his actions. One petition for clemency numbered nearly 30,000 signatures, and Hole's brother took to patrolling the streets of Bristol with a pony cart, on which were fixed a number of desks, trying to persuade people to sign.

As the date for his death neared, Hole reverted to his previously held Baptist faith and was visited every day by a deacon. He began to show signs of remorse for his crime, although he continued to protest to the very end that he had no memory whatsoever of actually committing the murder.

Hole was executed by William Marwood at Bristol Prison on 26 April 1875.

16

'IF SHE'S NOT DEAD, I'LL DEAD HER'

Narrow Quay, 1875

Philip Morris, aged 49, and his wife, Catherine should have been living a fairly comfortable life. He was an ex-soldier, having retired after serving almost twenty-five years in the Royal Artillery. At the time of his discharge in 1870, he had four good conduct stripes, not to mention the Sebastopol medal and clasps.

After leaving the forces, he obtained a position in Bristol's Custom House. On 24 April 1871, he married Catherine, becoming her third husband. Catherine worked as a tailor, so with her income and his salary, plus his army pension, the couple should have had no financial worries whatsoever. However, that was not the case. They shared a small, squalid rented room on Narrow Quay with Michael Cahill, Catherine's 9-year-old son from one of her previous marriages.

The reason for their poverty was alcohol. Catherine (and to a lesser extent, her husband) was in the habit of drinking 'great quantities of intoxicating liquor' and of pawning anything she could lay her hands on to raise money to support her habit.

On the morning of 5 April 1875, Catherine had already made three trips to the pub by 9 a.m., each time bringing back half a pint of whisky, which she shared with her husband. She then sent her son back to the pub for yet more alcohol. A message was sent to Philip's work to say that he was ill and would not be coming in that day and the two remained in bed drinking while Michael went out to play.

They were still in bed – although Catherine was fully dressed – when Mary Ann Lamb knocked on the door shortly after 11 o'clock. Mary Ann, aged 11, was the stepdaughter of Mr Gory, who owned the house in which the Morrises had their room. She had been sent to collect the rent and, when Morris asked how much was owed, he was astonished to learn that, despite him giving Catherine money on a regular basis, no rent had been paid for four months.

Having promised Mary Ann that he would sort out the problem of the outstanding rent in the next day or two, Morris turned to his wife and there was a brief argument between them about the arrears. A neighbour, Sarah Beckett,

68

Narrow Quay, 2007. (©N. Sly)

heard the argument and then saw Morris leaving the house, weaving drunkenly down the lane. He returned within five minutes and Beckett saw no more until young Michael came home at lunchtime.

When he did, he found his mother still in bed, covered in blood. There was blood on the foot of the bed and the room was even more disordered than usual, with chairs overturned, and a heavy wooden sleeve board, which Catherine used in her tailoring and usually kept by the window, lying on Michael's bed. It was covered with blood.

Michael ran to fetch a neighbour, Mrs Elizabeth Price, and Catherine was sent to hospital. There her skull was found to be fractured in five places and, after eight days, Catherine Morris died from her head injuries.

Philip Morris had been arrested at his sister's home in Park Lane for serious assault on his wife shortly after she had first been hospitalised. Having asked the arresting officer PC Capper if his wife was dead, he threatened; 'If she's not dead, I'll dead her.'

On Catherine's death, the charge against Philip Morris was upgraded to wilful murder and his trial opened on 12 August 1875 at the Bristol Assizes before Mr Justice Quain. Mr Norris represented Morris, while Mr Hooper and Mr Matthews acted for the prosecution.

The story that unfolded before the court was a sorry one of two alcoholics who endured a wretched marriage in which there was abuse from both parties. It emerged that Catherine had once thrown a bottle at her husband, causing a serious wound and, on another occasion, Philip had actually taken out a summons against his wife but had not followed it through. At the time of the attack on

Catherine, there were almost forty pawn tickets found in their room and, when asked by PC Capper why he had continued to live with his wife, Morris had replied despondently, 'How could I get away from the wretch?'

Various witnesses spoke for Philip Morris, giving him an excellent character reference. His unblemished military service was mentioned and it was intimated by his defence counsel that Catherine had been responsible for leading him into the 'habits of intemperance'. Several people spoke of him as a 'well conducted man', including his employer, Mr T.H. Fisher, who told the court of his recent promotion at work and described him as 'most inoffensive'.

The judge pointed out to the jury that, if they felt that Catherine Morris had somehow sufficiently provoked her husband, either by word or deed, resulting in him seizing the first weapon to hand, then the charge could be reduced from murder to manslaughter. However, since none of the near neighbours had heard any sounds of a violent quarrel, the prosecution took the position that there had been no such provocation and maintained that drunkenness could not be considered as an excuse for crime.

The jury obviously believed that the attack on Catherine Morris by her husband had been unprovoked, since they took only fifteen minutes to return a verdict of guilty of murder, although they did recommend mercy in view of Morris's previously unblemished character. With apparent regret, the judge put on the black cap and passed sentence of death on the prisoner.

However, within a short time, 14,230 people had signed a petition for Morris's reprieve, including all but one member of the jury. The missing jury member had travelled to Ireland following the trial but went as far as to send a telegram stating that he would have also signed the petition had he not been out of the country.

Morris was eventually granted a reprieve and his death sentence was amended to one of transportation. He was moved from Bristol Gaol to Pentonville Prison, from where he was later sent to the colonies for a life of penal servitude.

17

'LET ME LIE AND DIE HAPPY'

Having just settled down for the night, Jane Gillard of Wellington Road, St Paul's, was rudely startled into wakefulness when one of her lodgers, Eliza Distin, suddenly burst into her room. Wearing only her nightdress and bleeding heavily from a wound in her left shoulder, Eliza shouted, 'He have [*sic*] stabbed me! He have [*sic*] done it again. Go and see what he is doing!' She then turned abruptly and stumbled back towards her own room, with a terrified Mrs Gillard hot on her heels.

Eliza Distin and her husband, William Joseph Distin, usually known as Joe, had only been lodging with Jane Gillard for a week so their landlady knew very little about them. Had she had any inkling of Joe's history, she might well have been reluctant to rent him a room, but the Distins had seemed just like any other couple. Joe was gainfully employed as a cabinetmaker and Eliza was obviously devoted to her husband – to Mrs Gillard they had probably seemed like ideal tenants.

However, all was not as it seemed. For a start, Eliza and Joe Distin were not legally man and wife. Born Emily Eliza Tamlin and now calling herself Eliza Distin, Mrs Gillard's lodger was actually Emily Eliza Daniels, the widow of a steward on an ocean-going steamer. She had travelled with her late husband on many occasions, often working her passage as a stewardess, until he died in 1866 while in China.

Eliza had returned to Bristol where she had initially helped her sister to run a public house. She then changed careers and spent a year as a nurse at the Bristol Royal Infirmary before once again getting itchy feet and returning to working as a stewardess, this time sailing between England and America.

When she had finally had her fill of travelling, she returned to Bristol once more and moved in with her mother. Soon afterwards she met Distin and, by 1879, the two were co-habiting in rooms at Philadelphia Street.

Joe Distin was also not the respectable, steady man that he seemed at first glance. Once sufficiently gifted as a musician to be labelled a child prodigy, he had suffered a severe blow to the head while serving his apprenticeship and, from then on, his life changed completely. He became an alcoholic and, while fuelled by drink, totted up eight or nine suicide attempts and a large number of criminal convictions.

From 1866 onwards, he had violently assaulted his father and attacked his mother, which earned him twenty-one days' imprisonment with hard labour. A rampage of destruction at his mother's home gained him a further three-month prison sentence for destroying pictures and ornaments and a second attack on her person resulted in more hard labour and another three-month sentence. Over the years, he was frequently arrested for being drunk and disorderly, which almost always led to further charges of resisting arrest and assaulting the unfortunate policemen who tried to apprehend him. On one occasion, the charge of being drunk and disorderly was accompanied by one of exposing his naked person on the street.

His sisters, Emily and Rose, had also been victims of Joe's violent behaviour, as had Eliza. Only a few months earlier he had attacked her while drunk and had been charged with 'unlawfully cutting and wounding Eliza Daniels at 25 Philadelphia Street by stabbing her in the face with a knife with intent to do her grievous bodily harm.'

That act of violence not only earned him another prison sentence, but also got the couple evicted from their Philadelphia Street lodgings. Somewhat surprisingly, Eliza had welcomed him back with open arms after he had served his time and the two had found new accommodation with Mrs Gillard.

Now, on 27 September 1880, Eliza managed to stagger back to the small bedroom she shared with her 'husband' before collapsing at his feet with blood oozing from her shoulder. Mrs Gillard followed her into the room and turned on Joe crying, 'You have stabbed your wife and she is dying. What have you done, you villain?'

A stupefied Joe rose slowly from his chair and approached his wife, entreating, 'Eliza, dear, what have I done? What is the matter?' to which she replied, 'You have done for me this time.'

Concerned by the amount of blood that Eliza seemed to be losing, Mrs Gillard urged Joe to go for a doctor. Meekly, he put on his hat and coat, only to be stopped by Eliza who begged him not to leave. In exasperation, Mrs Gillard ran for help, returning with three neighbours, one of whom was immediately despatched to fetch a policeman while another, George Tilling, tried desperately to staunch the flow of blood from the injured woman by pressing wet rags to the wound.

Tilling asked Distin, 'What made you do this?' 'Oh, through jealousy', he replied casually. Meanwhile, Eliza had begun to panic when she realised that the police were on their way. 'Oh, don't fetch a policeman,' she begged. 'Let me lie and die happy.' Even as she uttered the words, PCs John Payne and Charles Prescott arrived at the scene of the crime. While Prescott set about getting Eliza to hospital, Payne immediately took possession of two bloodstained knives that had been found by the neighbours on the floor of the room.

Payne then turned his attention to Distin, telling him that he was under arrest and must accompany him to the police station. Predictably, Distin's reaction was one of aggression. 'It'll take a ****** sight better man than you to do so' he swore. Clearly intoxicated, he began to swing his fists and kick out at the policemen. He fought and struggled all the way to the police station and, once there, it took several officers to hold him down while he was searched.

Meanwhile, Eliza was admitted to Bristol Infirmary and taken to a ward, where she was examined by a surgeon. He found that she had a deep wound that began on her upper arm and passed through the muscles connecting her chest to her shoulder, severing a large vein. At the time, her condition was not thought to be life threatening but after a few days in hospital, it began to worsen, presumably as infection set in.

By 13 October, she was delirious, although she rallied to be sufficiently sound of mind to give a deposition from her hospital bed. In the presence of a magistrate, G.H. Leonard and his clerk, Mr Thomas Holmes Gore, Eliza stated that she could remember nothing of the stabbing, except that it was Distin who stabbed her while he was intoxicated. Distin, who had the legal right to be present at the taking of the deposition, then interrupted to point out that he had a cut over his eye and to ask Eliza if she had caused it. 'Certainly not' said Eliza, vehemently adding, 'I have not the heart to hurt a human being and certainly not you.'

Eliza told the officials that, on the night of the stabbing, she and Distin had visited a public house. They had been 'as happy as children' and had returned home for supper at about eight o'clock, in the company of several people whose names she did not know. Once at home, Joe had drunk some more beer.

Eliza said she did not know why Joe had stabbed her. She could only assume it was through jealousy, but could not recall talking or laughing with other men or doing anything else that might have made him jealous. When asked if the stabbing could have been accidental, she first said that she thought it was but then changed her mind, saying that Distin had deliberately run the knife into her shoulder.

On 16 October, Eliza Distin died. Mr Alfred Austin Lenden, the house surgeon under whose care Eliza had been while hospitalised, carried out a post-mortem examination. He found that the knife had in fact damaged a lung, causing the inflammation and infection that had ultimately proved fatal. Dr Lenden could see no reason why 39-year-old Eliza should have died other than the knife wound. At the subsequent inquest, presided over by the deputy coroner for the city, Mr E.M. Harwood, Eliza's death was deemed to be wilful murder.

William Joseph Distin was charged and brought before magistrates at the Bristol Police Court. He pleaded 'Not Guilty'.

The proceedings were presided over by Mr G.H. Leonard, one of the men who had taken Eliza's deposition (later in the hearing he was to suddenly fall ill and Mr George Wills took his place). Almost immediately, Distin began to argue that Eliza had not been of sound mind when her deposition was taken. Dr Lenden conceded that Eliza had been delirious on the night before her account of events was recorded, but maintained that she was capable of recognising people and of holding a rational conversation. He was absolutely certain that her mind was clear and that she knew what she was doing when she signed her statement.

Distin refused to accept this, stating that, in the course of giving her deposition, Eliza had asked for her tea. A woman in her right mind would not ask for tea at such a time, he argued.

The clerk of the court asked Lenden if he too had heard Eliza ask for her tea. Lenden said that he had, but that he had not considered her request a sign of mental derangement.

At this Distin interjected, claiming that Eliza had once told him that she suffered from heart disease. Lenden reiterated his findings from the post-mortem examination, at which he had found no evidence of heart disease and no reason why Eliza might have died other than from the consequences of the stab wound.

Next to address the court was George Ferris, who worked with Distin at Mr Payne's upholsterers at Castle Ditch. Ferris had left work with Distin at about one o'clock on the day of the stabbing and the two men had spent the afternoon in a pub, drinking steadily. Eliza joined them at about a quarter past five. At first, she had been rather angry with Joe because he had not been to work that afternoon, but her mood had soon mellowed. She had drunk a glass of beer then returned to the Distins' home for supper, which was washed down with more beer.

According to Ferris, Eliza had been taunting Joe about a 'fancy woman' in Philadelphia Street and had also slapped him lightly around the face. However, when he left the Distins' lodgings at about half past ten at night, the couple were on friendly terms, although definitely not sober.

George Tilling and Emma Bave, the two neighbours who had been summoned by Jane Gillard, gave their accounts of the aftermath of the stabbing, as did Mrs Gillard herself.

The question of the cut over Distin's eye was addressed, with the two attending policemen stating that neither had noticed a cut when they arrived at the scene of the crime. However, on the walk to the police station, Distin had been jostled and struck by an angry crowd of bystanders and, on his arrival, one constable had seen what he described as a slight scratch that could have been made by a fingernail.

Next to be called to give evidence was Thirza Bryant, the Distins' previous landlady. As she related her account of the first occasion in which Distin had stabbed Eliza, she was continuously interrupted by Distin, who, swearing and cursing, accused her of being a liar. Although warned by the court personnel, he continued to fire insults and accusations at Mrs Bryant, calling her 'the nuisance of Philadelphia Street.' 'What does she tell lies for!' he shouted, excitedly. 'Ain't [*sic*] I to have the law as well as her?' Soon the hearing degenerated into an extraordinary exchange of insults between Distin and Bryant, to the consternation of everyone but the two verbal combatants.

Although he argued long and loud about almost every word of testimony uttered by Thirza Bryant, it was to no avail and Distin was eventually committed for trial before Mr Justice Denman at the Winter Assizes. Mr Hooper and Mr Poole appeared for the prosecution, while Mr Valpy conducted Distin's defence.

The trial was virtually a repeat of the proceedings at the Magistrates' Court, with the same witnesses giving the same evidence. The only thing missing was the ferocious slanging-match between Distin and Thirza Bryant. Evidence relating to Distin's violent past was ruled inadmissible, so Bryant's testimony was very much shorter and less detailed and this time Distin managed to control his temper

Mr Valpy objected to the inclusion of Eliza Distin's deposition, but his objection was overruled. However, he did manage to draw a concession from Mr Lenden, the surgeon, who admitted that it was just possible that the stabbing might have been an accident if Distin had been holding the knife in his hand and had fallen drunkenly onto Eliza.

It was then left to counsels for the prosecution and defence to give their closing speeches. Hooper summed up the evidence for the jury and told them that their verdict could only be one of wilful murder, assuring them that the stabbing could not have been accidental and that he didn't believe that a verdict of manslaughter was appropriate in this case.

Valpy's view of the stabbing was naturally very different. Urging the jury to disregard the sensational headlines they may have read in the newspapers, he assured them that the stabbing was most likely the result of an accident. Distin had been drinking for several hours and it was probable that he had stumbled against Eliza with the knife in his hand. He reminded the jury that the surgeon himself had admitted that this was possible.

The judge then summed up the case. He too reminded the jury that anything they had heard or read about the case should be disregarded – treated 'like the idle wind' – and their verdict should be decided only on the basis of the evidence they had heard in court. He cautioned them about the reliability of Eliza's deposition, pointing out that she had been in a poor state of health when it was taken and had also contradicted herself as to whether or not the stabbing had been accidental. Yet, in his experience, he told the jury, it was not uncommon for a woman to try and shield her man, even when the injuries inflicted on her were sufficiently serious to later prove mortal.

He explained at great length that Distin's drunkenness on the night of the murder could not be seen as an excuse for his actions, saying that people could reduce themselves to the condition of beasts and yet still retain sufficient power to effectively wield a deadly weapon. Mr Justice Denman then told the jury that he had great faith in the testimony and opinions of Mr Lenden, the surgeon, a man whom he believed to be both highly qualified and also greatly experienced.

The jury retired for about twenty-five minutes, before returning with a verdict of 'Guilty of wilful murder', but with a recommendation for mercy.

'On what grounds?' asked the judge, to be told that the jury did not believe that the murder was premeditated.

When asked if he had anything to say why sentence of death should not be passed, Distin made no reply. The judge assumed the black cap and pronounced sentence and, having said that he understood the jury's recommendations, advised Distin not to rely on them to save his life. Instead, he urged him to spend his remaining time on earth repenting his conduct, reminding him that he had already been convicted of a violent assault on a fellow creature no less than eight times and that his previous assault on Eliza had warranted a far more severe punishment than it had ever received.

On 22 November 1880, William Joseph Distin received the severest punishment possible for the murder of Emily Eliza Daniels. It was said that he needed the administration of a stimulant in order to walk to the gallows but, unlike Eliza, who died a lingering and painful death as a result of his actions, death for 35-year-old Joe was almost instantaneous.

[Note: In various cotemporary accounts of the murder, the surgeon at Bristol Infirmary who attended Eliza is alternatively named as Lenden and Lindon.]

18

'WHERE IS MABEL?'

Avonmouth, 1897

On 2 January 1897, Jacob Rogers, the stationmaster at Avonmouth, spotted something unusual in a field some 200yds from the station. Fetching a field glass, he was surprised to see a little girl sitting alone on a plank at one of the rifle sheds on the Avonmouth range. He approached the dishevelled child, who sat motionless with her head in her hands, and asked her where she was from.

At first the child did not seem to hear the stationmaster's questions, but, when he persisted, she told him that she had come from Bristol with her cousin. She had lost her ticket and her cousin had run away and left her.

Rogers took her back to the warmth of his office, fetching a glass of water when she asked for a drink. He gave her some ginger brandy, then sent for some bread and cheese, but by now, the mysterious girl was unable to eat, seeming giddy and on the point of fainting. The manageress of the nearby Avonmouth Hotel arrived at the station and it was decided that the child should go with her to the hotel. A porter was despatched to the city police station to report the lost child.

Sergeant Coles and PC Wyatt went straight to the hotel where they found the child complaining of feeling unwell. Coles asked Wyatt to take her back to the station and to accompany her to the Bristol Royal Infirmary but by now, the little girl seemed to be completely exhausted and on the point of collapse. As Wyatt picked her up, with the intention of carrying her, he noticed that her underclothes were completely saturated with blood.

With the pale, cold child in his arms, Wyatt rushed to the surgery of Dr Falconer at Avonmouth Docks. When the doctor undressed and examined her, he found five large wounds on her torso, the longest of which was 6in in length. So severe were the child's injuries that portions of her intestines were protruding through the vicious cuts in her abdomen.

Sergeant Coles went to Clifton to arrange for a police ambulance to be mobilised to convey the girl to hospital. However, when he returned to the doctor's surgery, Dr Falconer had decided that such a journey was too dangerous.

The identity of the child had by now been established as 10-year-old Rosina Mabel Price, usually known as Mabel.

Avonmouth station. (Courtesy of Derek Fisher, Bygone Bristol*)*

Mabel lived in Dove Street, St George. Her father, William, was a labourer at Netham Chemical Works, where raw materials were processed to make sulphuric acid, quicklime and caustic soda. William shared his home with his wife and four children – Mabel, her elder sister Florence, and their two brothers, one aged 5 and the other, also called William, aged 19.

Mabel's mother had been mostly absent from home for the past eleven weeks, caring for her sick sister and making only occasional visits to her husband and children. Mabel's father had last seen his daughter as he was leaving for work early on the morning of Friday 1 January. When he returned home that evening, Mabel and her older brother, William were not there. While it was not unusual for the two siblings to go out together on occasions, the fact that they did not return by nightfall was worrying and prompted an extensive search of the area by the family. When there was no trace of the pair by Saturday morning, their disappearance was reported to the police at 6.15 a.m.

On Saturday evening, William was brought home alone by Ernest Bolson, a nearby neighbour. Obviously, the first question asked of him was 'Where is Mabel?' but, to the distress of the family, William didn't seem to know. All he would say was that she had run away from him at Avonmouth. Before he could be interrogated further, there was a knock at the door and William was promptly arrested.

By then, Mabel had been taken by ambulance to her aunt's house in Richmond Terrace, Avonmouth. Her condition was critical and she was not expected to survive, despite which, Mabel remained cheerful and made no complaints.

While Mabel's mother rushed to her daughter's bedside, her father went to Bristol Police Court to see his oldest son, William Lionel Price, brought before magistrates, charged with the attempted murder of his sister. However, it was established that the site of the attack on Mabel by her brother was on the border of two jurisdictions. Since Mabel was now at a house in Avonmouth, some 400yds outside the jurisdiction of the Bristol Police Court, magistrates Mr A.W. Price (no

Lawford's Gate Prison. (Courtesy of Derek Fisher, Bygone Bristol*)*

relation) and Mr A. Capper Pass determined that Price should be handed over to the Gloucestershire County Constabulary. He was taken to Lawford's Gate Prison.

As Mabel's condition was so grave, it was decided that a deposition should be taken from her at the earliest possible opportunity. Thus, Charles Thomas, a Gloucestershire magistrate and Mr Montague, clerk for Lawford's Gate Petty Sessions, were dispatched to Avonmouth on 4 January. They were accompanied by Superintendent Matthews, the chief of the County Constabulary and the accused, William Price, in the charge of Inspector Ricketts.

The men crowded into the small room of Mrs Hodge's house, where Mabel had been put to bed. Having first been informed of the seriousness of her condition and reminded of the importance of telling the truth, she then dictated a short statement.

She told of going to Lawrence Hill railway station with 'him' – at which she gestured towards her brother – and another girl. The three travelled by train to Avonmouth, then stayed in a field all night. Then, said Mabel, 'Willie cut me with a knife.' The other girl did nothing, but she and William left after Mabel had been cut. Mabel then sat in the field for about two hours until the man she referred to as 'the guard' found her. Mabel assured the assembled men that it didn't hurt her much when she was cut.

At this point, William interjected to ask if it was not towards morning, to which his sister replied that she couldn't tell.

The strain of giving her deposition and the fear of her brother, from whom the child visibly shrank away, took its toll on Mabel. Her condition gradually worsened until, at 6.15 p.m. that evening, she finally died from her injuries.

The cells at Lawford's Gate Prison. (Courtesy of Derek Fisher, Bygone Bristol)

The local newspaper of the day cited the fortitude with which she had borne her suffering and the reluctance with which she had revealed by whom her wounds were inflicted as a 'strange and pathetic feature of the case'.

Having been returned to Lawford's Gate, William Price was charged with the wilful murder of his sister, making no reply to the charge.

The inquest was held before coroner Dr E.M. Grace at the Parochial Schools, Avonmouth. Much to the coroner's displeasure, the police had mislaid a knife found in the possession of the accused and the inquest was adjourned to give them a chance of finding it.

Mabel's funeral took place on Sunday 10 January at Redfield Wesleyan Chapel and attracted large crowds. Her elm coffin, bedecked with flowers and wreaths, bore the inscription 'Rosina M. Price. 4.1.1897. Through the Cross to the Crown.' At around the time of the funeral, a rumour spread like wildfire around Bristol that the body of a girl had been found in Shirehampton Park, where it was believed that Mabel had spent her last night before being attacked. Police quickly denied the existence of a body, pointing out that not only had they found no remains, but that they had had no reports of any missing girls. The 'other girl' mentioned by Mabel in her deposition – if indeed there was one – was never identified.

William Price's trial opened at the Gloucester Assizes on 16 February 1897, before Mr Justice Day. He was charged with wounding Rosina Mabel Price on 2 January with intent to murder her and with the wilful murder of Rosina Mabel Price on 4 January. Mr Gwynne Jones and Mr Snagge appeared for the prosecution, with Mr L. Batten for the defence.

Price, described as 'a sturdy looking young fellow', stood in the dock completely unperturbed by his surroundings. When asked to plead, it was obvious that he didn't understand what was required of him, until prompted by Mr Batten to say, 'Not Guilty'.

Witnesses brought before the court testified to having seen Price and Mabel in various parts of Bristol on 1 January. At three o'clock, they were at Southmead, asking the way to Horfield; later they were seeking directions to Avonmouth, with Price specifically asking for the 'rifle butts', the place where Mabel received her terrible injuries.

Redfield Wesleyan Chapel. (Courtesy of Derek Fisher, Bygone Bristol)

On the morning of 2 January, Price was seen alone by a police officer near Avonmouth police station, a short distance from the rifle butts, and at lunchtime he was seen in Shirehampton by a woman who gave him food. That evening, he was spotted wandering aimlessly around by his neighbour, Bolson, who returned him to his home.

Much was made of Price's mental deficiencies. He was described as lifeless, apathetic, of feeble intellect and an imbecile. His father testified that his son had been 'strange in his head since he was a baby', a fact that was attributed to his mother having been shocked by the sight of a deformed child shortly before his birth. He had a very poor memory and had been bullied and teased throughout childhood.

Price had attended chapel and Sunday school regularly and his conduct at home was always good. Yet, he had been dismissed from the Gloucestershire Militia, which he had joined in 1896, as being mentally unfit for service. He had not worked for almost a year, his last job having been in a match factory. Price was obsessed with blood and it was said that one of his greatest pleasures was seeing horses killed. In addition, at the time of the offence, he had barely recovered from a severe bout of influenza.

In trying to establish his mental state in the time leading up to the trial, Price had been asked some simple questions but had failed to understand them. He had, for example, told his questioners that bacon was made from pig and mutton from pork.

When asked about the offence, all Price could say was that he had gone to Lawrence Hill, then he remembered nothing further except that there had been a girl there and then there had not. He denied knowing what had become of the girl but, when asked if he had cut her with a knife, after some hesitation, he admitted that he had. Asked if he was sorry, Price said that he was and that he wished he hadn't done it. He elaborated to say that something like gas had come in front of him.

Batten, speaking for the defence, maintained that Price was guilty of causing his sister's death but innocent of any intent to do so. Had he been in his right mind, he would have made an attempt either to conceal the crime or to escape; yet, he did neither. This, said Batten, was not a case where the prisoner could be forgiven, as he knew not what he had done.

In summing up, the judge pointed out that the mistake was allowing people like William Price, who he described as a congenital imbecile, to be free, rather than restrained in places specially provided for them. When the jury pronounced Price guilty, with the rider that they did not believe that he was responsible for his actions at the time of the attack, Mr Justice Day made it his business to ensure that Price was safely contained from that day on, during her Majesty's Pleasure.

[Note: In various contemporary accounts of the murder, Sergeant Coles is also referred to as Sergeant Cole. The age of Mabel's sister, Florence Price, is variously given as 14, 15 and 16 years old.]

19

'OH DEAR, MY POOR CHILDREN'

After Edward Pembery left for work early on the morning of 4 May 1900, his wife, Mary Ann, took the chance to have a few moments' lie-in before starting her chores. As she lay comfortable in her bed, halfway between sleep and wakefulness, one can only imagine her mounting terror as she heard heavy footsteps slowly coming up her stairs, accompanied by soft groans and gurgling sounds.

Suddenly the bedroom door flew open and a pale figure dressed only in a nightdress burst through it. Mary Ann instantly recognised the ghostly presence as her sister-in-law, Ellen Milsted, who lived next door with her husband, Henry and their six children: Henry (Harry), Louisa, Sidney, Frank, Elizabeth (Fanny) and Rosie. Ellen was clutching her throat tightly with both hands and a horrified Mary Ann noticed blood flowing between Ellen's fingers. As Mary Ann jumped out of bed to help her sister-in-law, Ellen slowly sank to the ground in a swoon. She never got up again.

Mary Ann called for Mrs Elizabeth Grainger, who, with her husband, lodged in the back bedroom of the Pemberys' house at 193 Pennywell Road. Mrs Grainger rushed into the room and saw Ellen lying on the floor, bleeding heavily from her throat, her nightdress soaked in blood. She immediately ran downstairs to seek help and, as she came out of the front door of the house onto the pavement, she spotted Henry Milsted leaving the neighbouring house, carrying his hat and coat. 'You have killed your wife!' she shouted at him. Henry calmly concurred that he had and told her that he was on his way to turn himself in to the police.

A passer-by, Thomas Paisey, witnessed the exchange between Mrs Grainger and Henry Milsted and immediately ran into 193 Pennywell Road to see what he could do to help. As soon as he entered the bedroom, he realised that Ellen was by now beyond any assistance, so he ran out again and set off up the road after Henry who was heading towards the city at a brisk pace. Paisey caught him up after about fifteen minutes and asked him, 'What have you done this for?' to which Milsted replied, 'I could not help it. I was bound to do it.'

Pennywell Road, 2007. (©N. Sly)

The two men walked peacefully along together, chatting quietly, as if out for a morning stroll. Paisey soon learned that Milsted had six children. 'You haven't hurt them as well?' he asked. Milsted recoiled in horror, 'God forbid' he said, assuring Paisey that he 'wouldn't hurt a hair of their heads.'

As Paisey and Milsted neared the police station, Milsted expressed a desire to see his son, Harry. Thinking that he might spot a policeman on the way, Paisey agreed to this diversion and the two men made their way to Howe's hat factory in Newfoundland Road where Harry worked. At the factory gates they knocked for Harry and, when he appeared, Milsted calmly told him, 'Harry, I have been and killed your mother.'

As Harry ran homewards, his father and Paisey continued their leisurely journey towards the police station. After a while, Henry complained of being thirsty and Paisey managed to procure a glass of water for him from a newsagent's shop.

They finally reached the police station at Bridewell Road where Paisey told Sergeant Foley, the duty sergeant, that he had brought Milsted in for cutting his wife's throat. 'That's quite right' agreed Milsted, and he was promptly taken into custody.

Meanwhile, back at Pennywell Road, Elizabeth Grainger had managed to find a policeman, Sergeant John Bridge, who had been patrolling his beat nearby with PC Field. The two officers hastened to no. 193, where they found Ellen Milsted still lying on the bedroom floor, covered in blood. A doctor had been sent for, but had not yet arrived, so Bridge arranged for a stretcher to carry Ellen to hospital.

Sending PC Field in pursuit of Henry Milsted, Bridge then went next door to no. 191 where he met Sidney Milsted. Sidney took the officer to his parents' bedroom and picked up a shoemaker's knife from the floor near the bed, which he handed to Bridge. (The Milsteds' two youngest daughters were still fast asleep in that same bedroom, completely unaware of what had happened.) Bridge noted that the knife was stained with wet blood and that there were drops of blood on the bedclothes, as well as a distinct trail of blood leading from the bedroom at no. 191 to the bedroom at no. 193.

Ellen Milsted arrived at the Bristol Royal Infirmary just before eight o'clock and was pronounced dead on arrival. Edward Stack, a house surgeon, subsequently conducted a post-mortem examination, observed by police surgeon George Myles. The two doctors noted the presence of a wound in Ellen's neck, starting about 2in below the lobe of her right ear. Although the wound was 2½in long, it was scarcely deeper than a scratch at one end and the doctors described it as being more like a single stab wound than a cut. It was agreed by the doctors that the knife found in the Milsteds' bedroom was capable of causing the injury. Ellen's windpipe had been completely severed, as had her jugular vein and carotid artery. Apart from the injury to her neck, Ellen also had an ulcer on one leg and considerable fatty degeneration of her liver. Neither doctor felt that these conditions were serious enough to cause her death and neither did they think that Ellen's wound was likely to be self-inflicted. They eventually recorded the cause of her death as haemorrhage from the wound to her throat.

An inquest was held into Ellen Milsted's death at the Crown and Dove Hotel, before Mr H.G. Doggett, the city coroner. The coroner first informed the court that he had received a letter from the governor at Bristol Gaol, telling him that Milsted was currently in the prison hospital receiving treatment for severe delirium tremens and that the prison medical officer had certified that Milsted would not be fit to attend the proceedings. In his absence, the coroner's jury returned a verdict of

Bristol Royal Infirmary. (Courtesy of Derek Fisher, Bygone Bristol*)*

wilful murder against Milsted and thus it was not until the case was heard at the Magistrates' Court that the full story of the relationship between Henry and his wife and the events leading up to her death became known.

Henry John Milsted, then aged 44, was a hunchback who worked as an outworker for Mr Ballinger, a Montpelier shoemaker. About fourteen years prior to her murder, his wife had taken to drink. She had spent every penny that Henry managed to earn on alcohol. Their children wore rags and the house was so squalid and filthy that five of the police officers investigating the killing had actually vomited at the stench.

Henry had tried begging and pleading with his wife to mend her ways, but nothing he did or said had any effect on her debauched behaviour. Periodically, Ellen would take all the money from the house, pawn anything that might have a monetary value, however small, and go off on a drinking binge for weeks at a time. While she was away from her husband, she would invariably earn the money for drink by working as a prostitute or by stealing.

On one occasion, Henry was forced to pay a fine she had incurred for theft. After this, Ellen promised him faithfully that she would give up drinking and, for almost a week, she stuck to her vow. Then, she went off on another drunken binge, which culminated in her being arrested and placed in Horfield Prison. Henry got word of her arrest, went to the prison and bailed her out but, before long, she was arrested again for theft and this time he was not permitted to pay bail and secure her release. Instead, she was sentenced to four months' incarceration in prison, leaving Henry with six children to care for, one a mere babe in arms.

Released from prison, Ellen came straight back to Henry, weeping bitterly, begging his forgiveness and promising him faithfully that, this time, things would be different. True, Ellen stopped stealing after serving her sentence, but, if anything, the drunken binges increased in frequency and intensity. She regularly pawned all the family's clothes and squandered the rent money on drink, disappearing for weeks at a time only to return when her money had run out. On one occasion, when Henry finally hardened his heart and refused to let her into the house, she threw stones at the windows until they shattered.

In desperation, Henry suggested that they set up a fried fish shop together, thinking that a business might distract Ellen from her cravings for drink. Ellen was delighted with this scheme, so Henry went ahead and, for around a month, his idea seemed to be working. Then, one night, Ellen got so drunk that she was unable to fry fish. A few days later, she was standing outside the shop and, when Henry asked his son to call her back inside, she was nowhere to be found. She had taken every last penny from the shop and disappeared on yet another drunken binge. Henry was forced to let the fish shop go.

He had not seen her for a month, when he accidentally bumped into her on the Horsefair, in the company of another man. Henry and Ellen talked for a while and Ellen soon discovered that he had given up the fish shop and demanded to know how much money he had received. Foolishly, Henry told her £5, at which she insisted that it was her fish shop and demanded the money.

She followed Henry home, all the while begging him to buy her a drink. Eventually, he relented, treating her to two glasses of beer and drinking a pint himself. By the time they reached home, she had somehow managed to persuade Henry to take her back again. Together they examined the newspapers for advertisements for houses and found one in Bean Street that Ellen thought would be suitable, if only she could buy some things for it. Henry parted with £3, with which Ellen bought some curtains and blinds, predictably spending the rest of the money on drink. Henry was forced to use his remaining £2 to cover Ellen's outstanding debts.

The couple lived together in Bean Street for about three weeks before their previous landlord at Pennywell Road offered them the fish shop back. Henry made some improvements to the property, including increasing the size of the boiler, but once again Ellen was discontented. Now getting drunk every single day, she insisted that Pennywell Road was too confining. One morning, she went out and did not return.

Having spent six months living in a brothel, she returned to Henry just before Christmas, asking for money. Henry agreed to give her board and lodgings if she would promise to behave for three months, but she was only after the price of a drink. Dramatically, she said goodbye to all of the children, swearing that she was going to kill herself but Henry met her again by accident three days later, this time in Milk Street when, once more, she begged to come home.

As it was so near to Christmas, Henry agreed, on condition that the children had no objections. He led her into the house and told them, 'I've brought your mother home.' When the children looked far from happy to see her, Henry told them that it was Christmas time and that they should all forgive and forget.

Christmas was spent fairly agreeably, but because Henry was on holiday from work, there was no money coming into the house. Ellen flew into a rage. She pawned the small gifts Henry had managed to buy for the children, as well as his one and only suit and spent the money on alcohol.

Between Christmas and the day of the murder, the pattern of behaviour continued. Ellen would leave to drink herself senseless, then return to her husband when she ran out of money, swearing to mend her ways. Describing his life as 'a burden', Henry finally snapped on the morning of 4 May 1900. After a night of quarrelling with his wife, during which she had abused him, hitting him at least twice and calling him 'every name she could lay her tongue to', Henry had seemed despondent when he got up on the day of the murder.

All the Milsted children seemed to place the blame for Ellen's death squarely on her behaviour towards their father. Although they recognised that he too had a drink problem, their impressions were that their mother had, quite literally, driven their father to drink. Harry recalled his father asking him on 4 May if he was going to work and, when Harry replied that he was, his father said sadly that, 'It seems so miserable after you have gone.' Henry also asked his son if he would help him out of his trouble and Harry, assuming that he was referring to rent arrears, assured him that he would.

Sidney corroborated his brother's evidence, telling the court that his mother spent every penny that Henry managed to earn on drink and that his father did everything he could to try and make her stop. He added that his father had been ill since Christmas and had been unable to work and that, on 4 May, he was still recovering from a bad bout of influenza. He also informed the court that his father's brother had been confined in a lunatic asylum for many years.

Fanny, aged 10, told of her parents' quarrel on the eve of the murder and of seeing her mother get up and go downstairs on the following morning. She had assumed that her mother was ill, a common situation in view of her prolific drinking, and had simply turned over and gone back to sleep.

The magistrates formally committed Henry Milsted to stand trial for the wilful murder of his wife at the next assizes and his trial took place in July 1900. Mr Douglas Metcalfe and Mr G.A.S. Garland prosecuted, while Mr G.A. Hawke defended, in spite of the fact that the accused did not have the money to pay him.

The court heard a repeat of the evidence given in the Magistrates' Court, with the addition of testimony about Milsted's attack of delirium tremens, experienced shortly after his arrest. The Chief Warder of Horfield Prison, Charles Morrell, told the court that two days after being admitted to the gaol, Milsted had 'got excited' and caused some damage to his cell. He had complained to the warders because they would not fetch him a pint of beer and, for his own safety, had been moved to a padded cell. He had quickly recovered and had since caused no trouble.

Dr Stack informed the court that delirium tremens was one of the many manias arising from drinking and that it was possible that a sufferer might not be as mentally stable as a non-drinker and so less able to resist acting on impulse.

Mr Douglas Metcalfe summed up the case for the prosecution, pointing out that there was little doubt, in view of the accused man's confession, that it was the hand of Henry Milsted that caused the death of his wife. What the jury must consider was whether there had been any premeditation and whether or not there had been sufficient provocation to reduce the charge to manslaughter.

Mr Hawke, for the defence, acknowledged that the prosecution had treated the case with moderation and humanity. He pointed out that, but for Milsted's confession, there was little evidence to connect him to Ellen's murder. He then addressed the question of provocation, telling the jury that there were times in life when people must make inferences in the absence of proved facts. He asked the jury to consider carefully whether or not they thought Milsted was insane at the time of the murder and to try to gauge the degree of provocation he was under when he struck the fatal blow with his knife.

The jury retired for almost three-quarters of an hour before returning a verdict of guilty of wilful murder against the accused, albeit with a strong recommendation for mercy on the grounds of the extreme provocation that Milsted had received over so many years.

It was not the judge's place to consider such a recommendation, although he agreed to pass it on to the relevant authorities. All that he could do at the conclusion of the trial was to put on his black cap and pronounce sentence of death on Henry John Milsted. As he did so, Milsted broke down and sobbed bitterly, his noisy crying almost drowning out the judge's words. 'Oh dear, my poor children' Milsted cried, entreating, 'Lord have mercy upon them.'

The authorities obviously heeded the jury's recommendation for mercy, since there is no record of his execution. Instead, he appears as an inmate of Dorset's Portland Prison in the census taken on 31 March 1901. Thus, it seems reasonable to assume that his death sentence was commuted to transportation for life. There is no record of the fate of his 'poor children'.

20

'EVERYTHING WENT BLACK'

Twenty-two-year-old Ada James was an enigma. Plump and dark haired, with a rather stern countenance, she could hardly be described as pretty, but despite her physical shortcomings, she seemed to attract men. Her apparent sensuality was in direct opposition to her regular attendance at a strict mission church, where restraint and purity for single girls were considered a requisite. Ada could neither be described as restrained nor pure, being a regular drinker and apparently also enjoying a healthy sex life.

Ada's fiancé, 23-year-old Edward Henry Palmer, known as Ted, enjoyed similar pursuits. He was a heavy drinker, favouring the 'spit and sawdust' back street pubs. A short man in stature, he had the broad-shouldered physique of an athlete and had indeed enjoyed some past success as a boxer. However, a once promising career in the ring was curtailed by failing eyesight and, robbed of the adulation that had come as a result of his sporting prowess, Ted grew unsettled. Life in Bristol no longer held any attraction for the restless young man, so he set off to seek his fortune.

Ted travelled to Canada where he stayed for almost twelve months, during which time he regularly wrote affectionate letters to his fiancée at home. He returned home to Albany Place, Montpelier, in 1912, shortly before Christmas, and he and Ada quickly took up where they had left off before his departure.

However, Ted's friends and family noticed some subtle changes in his character since his return. He had always been seen as cocky and pugnacious, often attempting to start fights in the public houses that he frequented. Yet, when the effects of drink had worn off, he was normally apologetic and contrite. And, when not in the pub, Ted could be intelligent, charming, eloquent and a considerate lover.

Ted had always been somewhat unbalanced. He was fond of carrying a revolver and had once fired it into a breadboard on the kitchen table. In an argument with his mother, he had pointed the loaded revolver at her and, in response to her comment of 'Go on then, Ted, kill me', had fired it up the chimney.

On Monday 27 January 1913, Ted had been drinking for most of the day before deciding to meet Ada after she finished work at the nail and button factory on St James's Square. However, Ada already had a prior engagement – the Bible Class Annual Tea at the Shaftesbury Crusade, which she had promised to attend with her brother, Alfred. Ted elected to wait until she returned.

He went for a walk – and most probably another drink – before returning to Ada's home in Union Road, St Philips, where he spent some time playing his mouth organ for Ada's younger sister. When Ada returned after about an hour, dressed in her Sunday best, the young couple set off arm in arm with the intention of walking to Narroways Hill.

The couple appeared to passers-by to be on the best of terms, but at some point in the evening, the pleasant mood vanished and one witness, Rosina Hancock, reported that the couple were quarrelling and 'talking nasty'. Unbeknown to Ada, the evening was about to get even nastier.

At about 8.30 p.m., Frederick Fry, a mason, almost tripped over what looked like a bundle of old clothes as he crossed from Lynmouth Road into Mina Road. A closer look revealed the bundle to be the unconscious body of a young woman lying on the pavement with her feet in the gutter, her face covered with blood.

Fry tried to make the young woman comfortable by placing a rolled up sack beneath her head, before running to a nearby shop in search of a glass of water for her. While he was away, another couple almost stumbled over the body in the darkness. This time, it was an off duty policeman, PC Parfitt, who happened to be out walking with his girlfriend.

Ada appeared to be regaining consciousness and was making an unintelligible gurgling sound. Kneeling on the pavement, administering what first aid he could, Parfitt searched his pockets until he found an old envelope and the stub of a pencil. With the last of her strength, Ada managed to grasp the pencil in her bloody fingers and scrawl four words on the paper: 'Ted Palmer Union Street'.

Although taken to hospital, Ada's throat was found to have been so viciously cut that her windpipe had been completely severed and she died as a result of her injuries in the early hours of that morning.

Palmer had left Ada on a footpath, bleeding and mortally wounded. She had somehow managed to make her way over a stile and through a wicket gate to the corner of Lynmouth Road before collapsing. PC Parfitt was able to follow a trail of her blood and, as he walked, his lamp picked up the sparkle of a woman's ring.

Having left his fiancée, Ted Palmer had visited several shops, buying stationery, presumably for the purpose of penning a suicide note. Finally, he had bought laudanum, an addictive opiate that, in those days, was widely prescribed for every ailment from colds and fever to menstrual cramps and heart disease.

Palmer downed the bottle of laudanum and wandered about aimlessly for some time, before deciding to call on his uncle for a glass of water. The police finally apprehended him in the early hours of the following morning, outside his uncle's home in Bean Street, still clutching the empty laudanum bottle in his hand. As he was escorted to Trinity Road police station, he complained of feeling weak and stated that he was going to die.

However, although Palmer was suffering from laudanum poisoning, he had ingested relatively little of the drug – certainly not enough to constitute a fatal dose. In his cell at the police station, the hardened ex-boxer wept like a baby, expressing genuine surprise that Ada had managed to reach Mina Road and asking police officers if they thought she had suffered much.

Since Ada and Ted were alone on the evening of 27 January, we only have Ted's version of events to rely on for an account of what had happened to Ada. According to Ted, he had once again mentioned his dissatisfaction with life in Bristol and expressed an intention to go travelling again, this time to the West Indies. He told Ada that he would send for her once he got established, but, in all probability, Ada had heard the same promises before when her fiancé had travelled to Canada.

Ada lost her temper, threw her engagement ring in his face and declared that, if Ted went, she would 'go on the town', saying 'I've done it before and I will do it again.' At this point, Ted stated that 'everything went black.'

He professed to have no memory of slitting Ada's throat with the second-hand razor he had purchased only the previous day for 10*d*.

Charged with Ada's murder, Ted's main concern seemed to be getting his spectacles returned to him. However, since he had already made one suicide attempt, it was decided that their return was unwise.

While Ted was incarcerated, Ada's body was laid out in the front parlour at her parents' home in Clark's buildings, where it was alleged that her father, Thomas James, made a considerable sum of money by charging people to view his daughter's corpse. Ada's funeral was held at Greenbank Cemetery, where a crowd of 2,000 people heard the minister who conducted the service describe the deceased as a 'Godly and virtuous young woman'.

Meanwhile, from his prison cell, Ted Palmer became a compulsive letter writer and, in a letter to Thomas James, he insinuated that Ada was anything but 'Godly and virtuous'. According to the letter, Ada had become pregnant and had been 'sent somewhere' by Palmer – presumably to an abortionist – and 'she got all right'. Having thus besmirched Ada's reputation, Palmer then continued to reassure James that his daughter was now a respectable married woman as he had legally married her in September 1911 and, if she happened to be 'in trouble' again when she died, then the baby was legitimate and he was the father. Palmer signed the letter 'from your daughter's broken-hearted husband.' Although Ada had been known to refer to Palmer in the past as her 'husband', no evidence of the alleged marriage was ever found.

Palmer's trial opened at the Bristol Assizes on 19 February 1913 before Lord Coleridge. Palmer, dressed in a smart grey jacket and trousers, waistcoat and black tie and now wearing his gold-rimmed spectacles again, pleaded 'Not Guilty' to the murder of Ada James. Yet, the letters he had written from prison were about to come back to haunt him. One, to his mother, seemed especially damning since Palmer had written 'It cannot be mended. I and Ada had a very bad row and like a flash I turned on her more like a wild animal than a human being.' However, the same letters were cited by the counsel for the defence, Mr J.G. Trapnell, as being indicative of his remorse rather than the words of a 'heartless, cold-blooded murderer'.

Corner of Lynmouth Road, where Ada James's body was found. (©N. Sly)

The prosecution maintained that Palmer's purchase of the razor immediately before the murder was evidence of premeditation. However, from the witness box, Palmer maintained that the purchase of the razor was a necessity since he had lost his old one (in fact his younger sister had hidden it, after he had crept into her bedroom and drunkenly threatened her with it). He had been too drunk to shave safely on Sunday; hence the razor was still in his pocket on Monday evening. The story of the opportune purchase of the razor might have been more convincing had it not been for the fact that Palmer had tried to redeem a revolver from a pawnshop on the same morning and, not having sufficient money for the ticket, had purchased a razor instead.

The court also heard that Rosina Hancock, the woman who had seen Ted and Ada quarrelling shortly before the murder, had been threatened with violence if she testified and it was hinted that other key witnesses had their silence bought.

In his summing up of the case for the jury, the judge pointed out that murder was not confined to cold blood but was sometimes committed in hot blood. After the jury took just fifteen minutes to find Palmer guilty of the wilful murder of Ada James, the judge sentenced Palmer to death by hanging, at which Palmer smiled sardonically, muttered a few indistinguishable words, then quickly descended from the dock to the cells below.

Palmer remained steadfast in the run-up to his execution, so much so that the prison governor asked that his absolute bravery be recorded. Even so, he lost over a stone in weight before being woken at six o'clock on the morning of 19 March 1913.

His solicitor's frantic efforts to gain a reprieve had proved fruitless and, just before eight o'clock, he was escorted by two wardens to the gallows where he was hanged by Thomas Pierrepoint, assisted by George Brown. His death was noted as instantaneous.

That Palmer slashed the throat of Ada James, the girl he professed to love, was indisputable. The reasons for the murder are less clear, since, of the two people involved, only one returned from the evening stroll to tell the tale. And what of Ada James? Were she and Palmer really legally married? Was this religious young factory worker also capable of 'going on the town' and engaging in prostitution? Her own brother, Alfred, testified in court that she had sometimes been the worse for drink and that she had received postcards from a man other than her fiancé, while Ted Palmer alleged that he had been told by people that her behaviour while he was away in Canada was far from abstemious.

All that can be reliably concluded is that Ada failed to anticipate the effects of her angry outburst on an unbalanced man, who had certainly been drinking heavily during the day. For this misjudgement, she paid the ultimate price.

21

'IF I HAVE DONE WRONG, I HAVE GOT TO PUT UP WITH IT'

Temple Meads, 1917

At 12.50 a.m. on 15 October 1917, Bristol Temple Meads station was already busy with soldiers rejoining their regiments after leave. As they awaited the arrival of the early morning train to London on platform five, most snatched the chance to spend a few last precious moments with their wives and sweethearts who had come to see them off on their journey.

It was a time of great turmoil and uncertainty in England. The First World War, now in its third year, was ultimately to claim over 900,000 British lives. More than six million British men were mobilised to fight overseas and, as the men were sent to the front, women were encouraged to take over their jobs. This new role was a far cry from life before the war, when few women worked and any employment available for those that did had been largely in domestic service. Many people felt at the time that this new way of life gave women far too much freedom and autonomy.

One woman believed to have enjoyed this new freedom was 27-year-old Bessie Cross who lived in Henry Row, Baptist Mills. Bessie's husband, Albert, aged 32, had been serving in France but, in spite of his long absence, she was six months' pregnant.

Private Albert John Cross knew about the pregnancy, since the child's father had spitefully written to him to tell him about his wife's 'carrying on'. James King of Barton Hill stated in his letter to Cross, dated 23 August 1917, that he had told Bessie that he would have nothing more to do with her, adding 'I do not know if your wife has written to you to let you know.'

Cross was understandably distraught at receiving this letter and immediately applied for compassionate leave to return to Bristol. He was told that he could not be permitted leave until October, so had to content himself with writing letters home.

93

Bristol Temple Meads station, early 1900s. (Author's collection)

Bristol Temple Meads station, 1966. (Author's collection)

He acknowledged King's letter, asking him, 'Why don't you be a man and stand by the woman you have ruined?' He continued, 'So far as I am concerned I only live for my poor little boys. I am finished with her but I am not going to see her ruined by a coward like you. I am her husband and I love her and I mean to protect her.' Albert signed his letter to King 'from Mr Cross whose home you have ruined.'

He then wrote to Bessie, enclosing a copy of his letter to King. His letter was vitriolic and bitter and was obviously intended to hit back at her for the pain her affair had caused him. He referred to Bessie as 'a cruel, lying woman' and wrote that he didn't care if he never heard from her again. He threatened to have the children taken away from her, writing, 'As regards the children, they will be far better off and will soon get used to being away from a cruel mother as you.' His letter to Bessie ended, 'You say that you can't starve, look to Mr King for pity, love for my boys xxxx'

Bessie's reply was heartrending. 'I confess I have done wrong' she wrote, 'but only with one man. This is the revenge that he said he would have. As you said, there is no forgiveness, I must go into the workhouse until I am out of my trouble... If you are going to take my little boys away from me, that will break their little hearts and mine...all I hope is that I die while I am going through it for I got [*sic*] nothing to live for now.'

Albert's reply was equally poignant:

Well, Bess, you know I have not got a hard heart but I must look after the welfare of my little boys. You say I might be happy when you are gone but Bess I still love you more dearly than I can tell you. Have I not told you times we have been talking quietly together how those dirty blaggards [*sic*] go hunting for women who have got their husbands away and what they do when they get tired of them but you would not listen to me. I have prayed to god [*sic*] more than once for you and the children and asked him to guide you. I hope you don't think, my dear I'm glad to hear this because I am broken hearted. I was hoping it was not true, but you confess it is true. I have taken steps to have my children taken away and you must know that I have shed many a tear as well as you and the children. You see, Bess, my love, if you listen to me I will be your friend as long as I live. If you knew what we have to go through you would have gone straight but the damage is done now, all the bitter feelings won't do any good. Ask god [*sic*] to take care of you and I will pray for you as well. Bess, try to be a different woman for the children's sake and mine. Love for my boys xxxx.

On 6 October 1917 Albert finally returned home and a lot happened during his ten-day furlough. Having expressed concerns about the moral welfare of his two young sons while in Bessie's care, Albert arranged a visit from Walter Hart, an inspector from the NSPCC. Albert had also made another request, asking James King to call at the house along with his wife. Mrs King's reaction to this visit can only be imagined, particularly as she and King had a family of nine children. James King, however, was later to say that he believed that Cross had forgiven him for his dalliance with his wife and that they parted on good terms.

Bessie and Albert had done a lot of talking during his leave and seemed to have largely reconciled their differences. Now Bessie had come to Temple Meads to say goodbye to her husband as he left Bristol to rejoin the 'Glosters' after his ten emotion-filled days at home. Suddenly, a shot rang out and Bessie slumped to the ground, dreadfully injured. After a moment's stunned silence, people rushed to her aid from all over the station, including Frederick Whitelock, a military policeman who, seeing Albert standing with a rifle in his hands, promptly arrested him. Albert willingly handed over his rifle to an employee of the Midland Railway Company and, as he was led away to the porter's room to await the arrival of the civil police, blurted out, 'I have shot my wife – she is in a certain condition by another man.'

Meanwhile, Ada Webb of the Women's Police Patrol managed with assistance to lift Bessie onto a nearby seat. Webb, who had been just feet away from the shooting, had heard Bessie crying; 'don't do it, don't do it' and saw her raising her hands above her head. Webb also saw Cross repeatedly fingering the trigger of his rifle, as if making up his mind whether or not to fire, then heard a loud crack, at which Bessie spun half around and fell to the floor, crying out that she was hurt.

An ambulance was summoned and Bessie was rushed to Bristol General Hospital, being admitted to the casualty ward at just after 1 a.m. Although she was restless and 'excited', she was still fully conscious, even though she had already lost a great deal of blood. Bessie was taken straight to the operating theatre, where attempts were made to locate the source of the bleeding and stop the flow, but in spite of the efforts of the surgeons, she died half an hour later.

A post-mortem examination revealed extensive internal injuries, including a shattered left kidney and three broken ribs and the cause of death was determined to be blood loss, coupled with shock. When Bessie's clothes were removed, numerous small fragments of metal were retrieved.

The inquest into her death was opened before Bristol city coroner, Mr A. Barker. The jury heard from Dr Cromie, senior house surgeon at the Bristol General Hospital, about the extent of Bessie wounds and the fruitless attempts to save her life. Dr Cromie also confirmed Bessie's pregnancy for the jury.

Bessie's mother, Mrs Hedder, spoke of visiting her daughter at home a few days before her death and of making a comment about her pregnancy. 'If I have done wrong, I have got to put up with it', said Bessie, adding that she had told her husband everything. When asked about the relationship between Bessie and Albert, Mrs Hedder stated that the couple lived together 'very unhappily'. While both were good parents to their children, their marriage floundered because each partner was extremely jealous and suspicious of the other.

Mrs Hedder admitted to the Coroner's Court that she had led an immoral life, but denied having been the one to introduce her daughter to James King. She stated that, having found out that King was a married man, she had asked her daughter to give him up but her request had not been heeded.

After Whitelock and Ada Webb had given their evidence, the jury then heard from Bessie Cross's lodger, Mrs Parry, who testified to having overheard her landlord and landlady discussing the pregnancy until the early hours of the morning. The coroner then adjourned the inquest.

When it resumed, the jury heard from PC Tyler, who had visited the Cross' home two days after the shooting and retrieved a packet of letters from behind a picture in the fireplace of the back bedroom usually used by Albert Cross. The letters were admitted as evidence and read by the coroner, one of them being a letter from James King to Bessie Cross arranging a meeting.

King was called before the jury and identified the letter as one he had written. Questioned by Mr E.J. Watson, who was representing Albert Cross, King admitted that he had been 'carrying on' with Bessie for about eight months and that he had bought her things. He was aware of her pregnancy and had written to Albert to tell him about Bessie's infidelities.

Watson was moved almost to tears in defending Cross, stating that one of Albert's letters to Bessie deserved to be preserved in gold. 'I have never in my life heard such a noble act of forgiveness as Albert Cross displayed', he told the court, referring to the exchange of letters between the couple in which Bessie begged for forgiveness and Albert professed his continuing love for her, even knowing of her infidelity.

The coroner's jury retired, deliberating for half an hour before returning with a most unusual verdict. In their opinion, they could only offer a verdict of wilful murder against Albert Cross, but stressed that the killing had been committed 'under great provocation'. The jury placed the blame for the murder squarely on the shoulders of James King, saying that he was responsible for all of Bessie's troubles. They found his conduct most reprehensible and felt that he was deserving of the 'severest censure'.

Mr Barker called King forward and told him that he fully agreed with the jury's sentiments. However, he had no choice but to commit Cross to be tried for the murder of his wife.

Cross's appearance before magistrates at Bristol Police Court on 30 October was nothing more than a prelude to his trial at the Bristol Assizes, which opened on 21 November before the Right Honourable Lord Coleridge. Having heard the evidence as given before the Coroner's and Magistrates' Courts, the trial jury listened to addresses from both the prosecuting and the defending counsels.

Mr F.E. Wetherley, for the prosecution, told the jury that, even if they didn't consider that there was enough evidence to warrant a verdict of murder, there was certainly sufficient evidence to show that Cross was guilty of culpable negligence, which equated to a verdict of manslaughter.

Mr E.H.C. Wethered, for the defence, stressed that Cross was a man of unimpeachable standing and, while he was serving in France, taking part in some of the most desperate battles fought there, King committed the basest action that a man could be guilty of in seducing Cross's wife. Describing King as a 'dastardly coward', Wethered asked the jury to consider what sort of man Cross was, referring them to the exchange of letters between Albert and Betty as an illustration of his good character. It was evident, said Mr Wethered, that Cross had forgiven his wife and also the man who had ruined his home. He conceded the seriousness of the words spoken by Albert Cross on his detention at Temple Meads, but maintained that 'I have shot my wife – she is in a certain condition by another man' could easily be the words of a man who was dazed with shock at what had just happened rather than those of a murderer. It was his opinion that a cartridge had accidentally been left in the rifle, which had no safety catch, and that Cross had either forgotten about it or just didn't know that it was there.

In his summing up of the case, the judge appeared noticeably favourable towards the prisoner. 'The law is not the cold, callous, indifferent matter some people would have you believe', he told the jury. He declared that the letters produced in court would evoke sympathy for the accused in even the most callous of persons and advised the jury to make allowances for the soldier's life that Cross had been living when reaching their decision. Feelings towards death and injury were blunted by service on the front line, he said, so they must apply different rules to the prisoner than they would to an ordinary individual.

Accordingly, after deliberating for approximately ninety minutes, the jury returned a verdict of 'Not Guilty' and His Lordship ordered that Albert Cross be discharged immediately. Cross was freed to return to France and continue fighting for his country.

We will never know whether Albert Cross intended to shoot his wife on that October morning, or whether her death was a tragic accident or perhaps even a playful gesture that went terribly wrong. It is easy to imagine Cross saying jokingly to his wife as they parted that he would shoot her if she misbehaved again and raising his gun, unaware that it was loaded. Yet, at the same time, it is more difficult to believe that an experienced soldier, who was staying in a house with his two young sons, would not have made absolutely sure that his gun was safe while he was at home.

22

'I HAVE PUT HIM IN A POSITION THAT HE WON'T COME BACK AGAIN'

Brislington, 1923

[This is the account of the murder of George William Cooper by his son, also called George William Cooper. To avoid confusion, George Cooper Senior is generally referred to as Cooper and his son as George.]

On Thursday 6 September 1923, George Cooper Senior left his work as a pattern maker at Sampson & Sons Ltd, spent some time working on his allotment and then shared a drink with a friend, eventually heading home at about 8 p.m. Two days later, Cooper's wife visited Sampson's in some distress. She told managing director Frank Sampson that her husband had returned home on the Thursday evening and immediately started an argument, during which he had become violent and abusive towards her. Her son, also called George, had defended her, at which her husband put on his coat and left the house. According to Mrs Cooper, he had not yet returned.

Mrs Cooper was no stranger to the management at Sampson & Sons. On two previous occasions, she had visited the premises complaining that her husband was engaged in 'carrying out an intrigue' with Mrs Goodman, an office cleaner at the firm. Having examined company time sheets and noted that Cooper frequently claimed overtime for Saturday afternoons when Mrs Goodman was working, and that he appeared to have paid for Mrs Goodman to go on the works outing, Mr Sampson dismissed his cleaner on 4 September.

George also worked at Sampson's and, having told the firm that he didn't believe that his father would be returning, he eventually took over his father's more senior job.

Montrose Avenue, Brislington. (©N. Sly)

Prior to 59-year-old Cooper's unexplained disappearance, he gave every outward impression of being the head of a happy, respectable family. He and his wife, Louisa, aged 57, lived in Montrose Avenue, Brislington. George, aged 37, shared an unusually close relationship with his mother and, when he married in 1921, he and his new bride moved into his parents' home. Soon, the first grandchild was born, a boy whom Louisa doted on. By 1923, George and his wife were expecting their second child and in June of that year, George's wife went to stay with her own mother in Cheddar for the confinement, leaving her son to be looked after by his grandmother. She had intended to return to her husband in September, but stayed at her mother's home until just before Christmas. A lodger, Mr Baker, completed the Cooper household.

However, all was not what it seemed. Cooper was a womaniser, having enjoyed several extra-marital affairs, most of which had eventually come to the attention of his long-suffering wife. He had even once invited one of his mistresses to stay at his home, insisting that his wife wait on her. (He was later to be described by a solicitor, Mr Watson, as 'a lascivious leper, an unrepentant profligate, who boasted of his profligacy.') Although a man of good character, Cooper was known for his violent, hair-trigger temper and had a penchant for throwing things rather than engaging in calm, rational discussions. He often went on rampages of destruction at home, smashing crockery and ornaments. A surly man, he was frequently abusive towards Louisa, who had often been seen sporting a black eye. In the past, Louisa's brother had threatened on many occasions to give him a good hiding, but Cooper would not accept any criticism about his treatment of his wife, instead bragging blatantly to anyone who would listen about his frequent infidelities.

George Cooper and his mother, Louisa. (Courtesy of Bristol Central Library Archives)

In the absence of his father, George became the man of the house and, when his mother complained to the landlord that some floor joists needed replacing, he took it upon himself to do the job, being reimbursed by the landlord for the cost of the timbers, but refusing any payment for his labour. On 10 January 1924, with no sign of Cooper's return, George officially took over the tenancy of the house in Montrose Avenue.

After Cooper's disappearance from home, George and his mother gave differing accounts of his absence to different people. Some were told that he was working away from home, others that he had left with a woman. It wasn't until January 1924 that someone was finally told the truth.

George visited his uncle and aunt, George and Elizabeth Blackburn. When asked about his father, George said that there had been an argument and added, 'I have put him in a position that he won't come back again.' When pressed by his aunt to explain himself, George admitted that he had killed his father.

This confession put the Blackburns in a rather awkward position and, the next day, they sought advice from a friend, George Paul, a fried fish shop owner who was also an ex-policeman. Paul realised that he had no alternative but to go to the authorities with his knowledge of the fate of George Cooper Senior and, as a result, both George and his mother were arrested and charged; George with the murder of his father on or about 6 September 1923 and Louisa with being an accessory after the fact. Meanwhile, police moved into the neat and tidy house on Montrose Avenue and began a thorough search of the premises, paying particular attention to a back room in which George had only recently completed his repairs to the floor joists. There, buried 5ft beneath the floorboards, they found the

Brislington Cemetery, 2007. (©N. Sly)

decomposing body of George William Cooper Senior. It was fully clothed apart from missing trousers, wrapped in sacking and covered with lime and tar. Up until the discovery of the body, the room had been used as a sitting room by George, his wife and their two young sons.

Louisa and George were remanded in custody pending a full search of the house; George at Horfield Gaol, his mother at Cardiff. Meanwhile, Cooper's body was removed to Keynsham workhouse, where Dr McClelland and Dr Cochrane carried out a post-mortem examination. Preliminary findings indicated that the deceased had numerous severe head injuries, probably caused by a small hatchet that had been found in a shed in the back garden, any of which would have been sufficient to kill him. Although the body was by now very decomposed, the doctors gave the cause of death as fractures of the skull and Cooper's remains were released for burial in Brislington Cemetery. The inquest into Cooper's death, which had been opened by Dr Samuel Craddock, the coroner for North Somerset, was adjourned.

When the inquest was resumed on 18 February, it was to the shocking news that the Home Office had ordered the body to be exhumed so that the celebrated pathologist Sir Bernard Spilsbury might examine it. With only one policeman, two gravediggers and a newspaper reporter to oversee the proceedings, the grave was opened in the early hours of the morning of 17 February and Cooper's body was removed and placed on a cart to be transported to the Bristol City mortuary. There it was met by the city coroner, Mr Barker and Superintendents Ford and Tanner of the Somerset and Bristol Police respectively. Dr Hedley Hill, who was representing the interests of the accused, arrived a little later, by which time

Spilsbury had already made a start on his examination. In the presence of the two doctors who conducted the original post-mortem, Spilsbury spent a total of three hours at the mortuary.

The solicitor defending George, Mr Watson, protested strongly that he had been given no notice of the exhumation and was told by the coroner that he had been informed at short notice by the Department of Public Prosecutions that it was to take place and had accordingly been asked to adjourn the inquest. Watson again protested in vain that he had had no opportunity to cross-examine the doctors who carried out the original post-mortem examination but despite what Watson called 'irregular proceedings' by the Crown Authorities, the inquest was again adjourned until 5 March. When it resumed, Watson was still protesting the injustice and irregularities and was further angered when the coroner adjourned the inquest again, this time until 24 March, so that Spilsbury might complete his investigations.

Spilsbury first presented his findings at police court proceedings at Keynsham. He described opening the coffin with the name-plate 'George William Cooper' and observing a man's body, which had a shrunken appearance and was contaminated by fragments of clay and lime. On examination of the dead man's skull, he noted nine separate injuries where the skull had been completely cut through.

He believed that all but two of the wounds had been caused by a weapon with a cutting edge slightly less than 4in long. Just the extreme point of the weapon, rather than the whole of the cutting edge, might have caused the other two wounds. Any of the wounds, which Spilsbury described as having been inflicted with 'extreme violence', would have immediately rendered Cooper unconscious, meaning that the others must have been inflicted after the deceased had fallen to the floor. It was not possible to state whether the majority of the injuries had occurred before or shortly after death, but Spilsbury pinpointed the cause of death as haemorrhage from the wounds.

Mr Watson, acting for the defence, then had several tools brought into the courtroom, asking Spilsbury to look at the two shovels and the pickaxe used in the exhumation of the body. Watson suggested that these instruments could have caused the numerous skull fractures and head wounds. Spilsbury examined them closely, then stated that he would like to compare them with the deceased's skull. Proceedings were adjourned to allow him the opportunity to do so.

Meanwhile, the coroner's inquest re-opened on 24 March, with Watson still protesting about being unable to cross-examine the medical witnesses. The coroner's jury were permitted to question Sergeant Carter, the arresting officer, about a statement that George had allegedly made when he was first apprehended.

George had stated that when his father arrived home on the evening of 6 September, he had asked where his wife was, then immediately began to quarrel with his son. George had described the house as being in disarray – there were marks of broken eggs on the door and pieces of smashed crockery on the floor. When George asked his father the reason for the mess, Cooper had replied; 'When your mother comes home, she will know what the ******* reason is.'

George had immediately flown to his mother's defence, telling his father that he wasn't going to touch her. There followed an argument about whom Cooper might bring to the house, with Cooper saying that he could bring anyone he liked and George, obviously referring to Mrs Goodman the cleaning lady, protesting that he could not bring anyone from South Street.

According to George's statement, Cooper had allegedly shown him the door, saying that there could not be two bosses in one household. Then, when George refused to leave, Cooper had picked up a cast-iron fire ornament and made as if to throw it at his son. George had dodged the missile and kicked his father on the thigh, causing him to fall to the floor.

With his father's curses still ringing in his ears, George went into the living room and began to play the piano. He heard his father go into the shed in the back garden, then, shortly afterwards, he caught a glimpse in the mirror of his father entering the living room behind him. As Cooper rushed into the room, pulling a hatchet from beneath his waistcoat, George jumped up and dived at his father. The two struggled for some time before George managed to wrest the hatchet from his father's grasp. Feeling that it was his father's life or his, he struck out with the weapon, hitting his father a blow on the head.

When his mother returned home later that evening, she was told by George that he and his father had rowed and Cooper had gone out. Only after his mother had gone to bed did George, after considerable reflection, feel the need to tell her what had happened. He went to her bedroom, sat on the side of her bed and confessed to her that he had killed his father.

At this point, while police were taking the statement, Mrs Cooper had suddenly burst into the room in hysterics, crying: 'I did it, I did it. Have mercy on my son.' The coroner's jury wanted to know if the confession by George had been made voluntarily and were assured that it had.

Watson then pointed out that there was a discrepancy in Superintendent Tanner's copy of the statement – the only one that was signed. In Tanner's copy, George had allegedly said: 'I killed him and told my mother she was not to go into the room until I had all the place in order and the boards down again.' In Carter's copy, the wording was slightly different, reading 'until *she* had all the place in order and the boards down again.'

Finally, Watson was at long last allowed to question Dr McClelland, although when he began to ask questions of a pathological nature, the coroner promptly protested that his questions were irrelevant and a waste of time. He then adjourned the enquiry for lunch, after which he asked the jury whether they felt that the cross-examination by Watson on pathological conditions should be allowed. The foreman of the jury, while commending Watson on his handling of the case, determined that they could not accept his cross-examination, at which Watson bowed to the jury's decision, while still protesting at the exclusion of his questions.

The jury decided that it was unnecessary to call Sir Bernard Spilsbury since it was evident that the cause of Cooper's death had been head wounds and it was left to the coroner to sum up the evidence, which he did to a background of sobbing from Louisa Cooper.

After the coroner's summary, there was a final protest from Watson that he had not discussed malice aforethought. The jury then withdrew for about an hour and a half before returning with a verdict of wilful murder against George. They added a rider to their verdict that they were of the opinion that he had been under a great deal of provocation and had committed the murder in the heat of passion. Maintaining that the question of manslaughter must be left to another court, the coroner instructed that George be tried for the wilful murder of his father.

George and his mother appeared before Keynsham magistrates on 4 April. Despite vigorous arguments from Mr Watson in which he accused the police of 'cooking' the statements of both defendants and complained that the conduct of the Somerset Police and the Home Office had 'cast an indelible stain on the fair figure of justice', both were committed for trial.

The trial opened at the Somerset Assizes in Wells on 29 May 1924 before Mr Justice Shearman. George was indicted for his father's murder, while Louisa stood accused of 'receiving, harbouring and maintaining her son, George William Cooper, well knowing him to have committed a felony.' S.H. Emmanuel KC and Percival Clarke conducted the prosecution, while Holman Gregory KC and F.E. Wetherley appeared for the defendants, both of whom pleaded 'Not Guilty' to the charges against them.

The court heard from Cooper's employer, Frank Sampson, who repeated the evidence he had given in the Coroner's Court. The Coopers' lodger, Mr Baker, spoke of a discussion with Cooper about his infidelities, and there were then some legal arguments as to the validity of Mrs Cooper's interjection of 'I did it', made while police were taking a statement from her son.

Mr Justice Shearman ruled that this exclamation was not admissible, since Mrs Cooper had not been under caution when it was made. Inspector Tanner agreed that Mrs Cooper was in an hysterical state at the time.

The police gave evidence that George had insisted that the murder was not committed with malice aforethought; rather, he had acted in self defence, fearing that his father was about to kill him. George himself repeated this assertion from the witness box, admitting to having killed his father but otherwise sticking to his original statement. His mother did not give evidence.

Counsel for the prosecution addressed the jury telling them that, if they were fully satisfied that George had killed his father by hitting him over the head with a hatchet, then it was their duty to find him guilty of murder. His speech was interrupted by tearful exclamations from Mrs Cooper, who first implored the jury to 'Save him, save him!' and then screamed 'It is not true! Oh! It is not true!'

Mr Gregory, meanwhile, defended Mrs Cooper by suggesting to the jury that she had not known that George had killed his father. With regard to George, Gregory stressed that the fatal blows had been struck in self-defence while George feared for his own life.

In summary, Mr Justice Shearman instructed the jury that the cases against the two defendants must be considered separately from each other. Where George was concerned, he told them, there were three alternative verdicts – they could find him not guilty if they felt that he had acted in self-defence, guilty of manslaughter if they felt that there was no premeditation, or guilty of murder.

The jury retired for three quarters of an hour before returning with their verdicts. They found George guilty of manslaughter and Mrs Cooper guilty of being an accessory after the fact.

Turning to a tearful Louisa, the judge told her that he did not feel that he could be too hard on her for protecting her own son. Since she had already served eight weeks in prison, he determined that she should be given time served and bound over. 'Try to forgive my son', Mrs Cooper begged him as she was led from the court to be released. The judge then announced his intention to give some more thought to the sentencing of George Cooper Junior and to defer his decision until the following day.

The judge eventually decided to sentence him to seven years in prison.

After serving his sentence, George was released from prison and continued to live in the Bristol area. He is believed to have died in 1984, by which time he was well into his nineties.

23

'HURRY UP, GILBERT'

The shops were open later than usual in the busy run-up to Christmas, so, on Friday 15 December 1924, Mrs Amos, who lived with her husband, Herbert, and their three sons in Burchill's Cottages, Staple Hill, took the opportunity of doing some evening shopping. Herbert, who was a general labourer on the railway, had already agreed to meet up with friends for a drink that evening, so the children were left at home in the charge of Willie, the eldest boy.

Mrs Amos and her friend Mrs Green met up with Herbert at about 10 p.m. and Mr and Mrs Amos then walked home together. At about 10.30 p.m., Mrs Amos went upstairs to check on the children. Eleven-year-old Willie and 2-year-old Walter were sleeping peacefully in their beds but there was no sign of Gilbert, aged 8½.

When questioned by his worried parents, Willie said that there had been a knock on the door at about nine o'clock. When Willie had answered, the man standing on the doorstep said that he had come from their Aunt Lizzie's and that she wanted Willie to go to her house as she had something for him.

Conscious of his responsibilities as a babysitter, Willie had explained that he was unable to leave the house, since he was in charge of his younger brothers. However, Gilbert had promptly offered to go in his place. He had been preparing for bed when the caller arrived, but now he quickly replaced his boots and set off with the man towards his aunt's house. As Willie watched them walk away, he saw Gilbert bend down to tie his bootlace, at which he was prompted by the man to 'Hurry up, Gilbert.'

Feeling tired, Willie didn't wait up for Gilbert's return but instead put Walter to bed then went to sleep himself, only to be woken later by his worried parents asking him where Gilbert was.

The boys' Aunt Lizzie, Elizabeth Morton, lived only a short distance away in Portland Street. When Gilbert's parents arrived at her house, she denied both having seen him and having sent any message – in fact, she had been out herself all evening. Mr and Mrs Amos continued to search high and low for Gilbert until about 2 a.m., when they were told to contact the police. When they did, it was to receive the worst possible news – a body had been found.

Staple Hill. (Courtesy of Derek Fisher, Bygone Bristol*)*

Herbert Amos was taken to the police station at Fishponds to identify the body. Gilbert Caleb Amos, described by his grandmother as a 'sturdy, jolly little chap', had been strangled with a black knitted tie and also sexually assaulted; sodomised when either unconscious or dead. A slit had been cut into the navy blue knickerbocker trousers he was wearing.

The body had been found in Cozen's Field, which lay close to Staple Hill railway station. At Soundwell Road, near to the home of Elizabeth Morton, lived Mr and Mrs Bressington with their son, 21-year-old William. William had recently returned to live with his parents, having been away from home for a few weeks, working in London. On the evening of the murder, Mrs Bressington inexplicably became worried about him, a concern that prompted her to seek out her husband, Charles. Together with a family friend, William Britton, Charles went out looking for his son, eventually finding him close to the Derham Boot Factory.

Exactly what was said at that meeting was later to be much debated. William Bressington allegedly said either, 'I have done it, Daddy' or 'I have done wrong.' He then led his father and Britton to a corner of Cozen's Field and pointed out a child's body. William Britton went to examine the body, returning to say that it was a little girl and the body was cold. An enraged Charles Bressington flew at his son and pinned him to the ground, while Britton rushed to the nearby station and summoned assistance. The first to arrive at the scene of the murder were two lantern-bearing porters, quickly followed by a policeman, Constable Hawkins. After handcuffing William Bressington, Hawkins wrapped the child – now correctly identified as a boy – in his overcoat and gave artificial respiration until Dr M. Barber arrived and pronounced life extinct.

At this, the officer turned his attention back to William Bressington, who had by now collapsed onto the ground. He was dragged upright and escorted to St George police station, where he was formally charged with the boy's murder. Bressignton was subsequently moved to Bridewell Street police station and brought before the magistrates the following morning. His should have been the first case heard that day but, as he was being brought up from the cells, he collapsed and had to be revived. He was later half carried into the dock and supported between two police officers, Sergeant Thick and Constable Brown, while the charges against him were read.

The inquest was opened on the following Tuesday before Bristol coroner Mr A.E. Barker and quickly adjourned for three days. Young Gilbert Amos was buried on the Thursday in Mangotsfield Cemetery, his small body transported on a hand bier along roads lined with hundreds of people. At his school, the children stood silently in the playground to pay their respects.

William Bressington attended the inquest when it resumed, sitting quietly, his head bowed and his body visibly shaking, as Herbert Amos was called to give evidence. Amos identified the slashed knickerbockers that Gilbert had been wearing and confirmed that the black tie used to strangle the boy had not belonged to his son.

Bressington's father had apparently been so outraged at his son's deeds that a fight had broken out between them when the body was discovered and Bressington Senior had to be physically restrained. However, he denied having said, 'This is the bastard who killed the kiddie' to the first police officer on the scene. However, Police Constable John Hawkins insisted that those very words had been spoken. Hawkins described taking a signed statement from Bressington in which he confessed, 'Yes, I murdered him. I put a tie round his neck.' Mr Stredwick, representing the accused, objected to this statement, fearing it might be prejudicial towards his client at the trial.

Two witnesses then testified that Bressington had mentioned the presence of another party to the murder, one witness believing the third person was called 'James', the other, 'Charlie'.

Bressington's trial began at Bristol on 16 February 1925 before Mr Justice Roche. Bressington immediately pleaded 'Guilty' to the charge of wilful murder and Roche had to intervene to say that such a plea was not normal practice. A plea of 'Not Guilty' was then entered.

The prosecution, led by S.H. Emmanuel, outlined the events of 15 December 1924 and, at this point, the possibility of an insanity plea was raised. If Bressington had said to his father 'I have done wrong', then the jury must ask themselves firstly whether he knew the nature of his acts and secondly, whether or not he realised that they were wrong. Emmanuel told the court that he expected the jury to answer 'Yes' to both questions.

Herbert Amos, his son Willie and Elizabeth Morton – Aunt Lizzie – all recounted their memories of the night of the murder, and then it was the turn of Charles Bressington to take the witness stand.

Bressington maintained that his son had made no mention of wrongdoing but had actually said, 'I have done it, Daddy. I have done it. I cannot tell you but I will take you to the place and show you.'

He described his son as being 'funny from a baby onwards', saying that, since early childhood, he had frequently complained of pains in his head. He reeled off a long list of close relatives who had died insane, including William's grandfather, uncle and cousin and told the court that his son was in the habit of wandering off and was frequently returned home by the police. William Bressington was well known in the area for his odd behaviour – he often wore women's clothing and make up in public and on his arrest had been carrying face powder and a powder puff in his pocket.

When he was 15 years old, William had attempted to commit suicide by taking poison. He had run away from home and enlisted in the Berkshire Regiment of the army in August 1919 but had been quickly discharged because of what was described as 'feeble-mindedness'. In the past, he had been known to suffer from fits.

After leaving the army, he had run away from home again, leaving his family with no idea of his whereabouts until he was arrested in July 1921 for stealing from empty houses.

The medical superintendent of Horfield Prison, Dr William Cotton, testified that the prisoner had been in his care previously in 1921, when he had perceived him to be 'unbalanced' rather than insane. Cotton said that Bressington, who was being closely observed in the prison because of a suicide attempt, always appeared rational, lucid and under control.

However, other witnesses drew a rather different conclusion. Police Constable Trinder, based at Staple Hill police station, had once found Bressington lying in the middle of a road, flailing his arms and legs and repeatedly shouting, 'They are coming over!' When Trinder approached to assist Bressington, he resisted violently and tried to bite the officer.

Dr Robert Phillips of Northwood Asylum had spoken to Bressington at length and the accused had answered in a detached manner. Phillips felt that Bresington was a mental defective who could not differentiate between right and wrong and that his family history of insanity and acute mania had some bearing on his condition. He told the court that he personally would have no hesitation in certifying the prisoner insane.

Another doctor, Dr R. Barton-White, the medical superintendent at the Bristol Mental Institution, had also noticed a detachment and lack of emotion when he had discussed the murder with Bressington shortly before the start of the trial. He too felt that the accused knew that he was taking Gilbert's life, but did not understand the difference between right and wrong.

In his summing up, the judge told the jury to consider whether the prisoner was guilty of murder or, as suggested by the defence, guilty but not responsible for his actions.

The jury took less than an hour to return with a guilty verdict, although with a recommendation of mercy on the grounds of Bressington's weak mentality.

Mr Justice Roche assured them that their recommendation would be 'considered in the right quarter' before passing the death sentence, at which Bressington began to sob loudly and had to be supported as he left the court.

Yet the recommendation for mercy was obviously not acted upon, since Thomas Pierrepoint executed 21-year-old Bressington at Bristol on Tuesday

31 March 1925. He was undoubtedly responsible for the death of young Gilbert Amos, but, given his mental state at the time of the killing, his execution was thought by many at the time to be unwarranted.

[Note: In contemporary accounts of the murder, the location of the body of Gilbert Amos is variously described as Cousins' or Cousin's Field. The age of William Amos, brother of the deceased, is given as both 11 and 12 years old and William Bressington's execution is said to have taken place either when he was 21 years old or on the day after his twenty-second birthday.]

24

'AND YOU TOO, YOU RAT'

Hanham Woods, 1935

The newspapers of the day gave the impression that the collection of homes in Hanham Woods was little more than a shanty town. However, this was far from the truth. By May 1935, numerous families had established thriving smallholdings within the woods, some farming pigs, others keeping poultry and one couple even running a small shop on the banks of the river Avon, from which they sold refreshments to those people who came walking on the riverbanks or boating.

One such family were Henry Nott, his wife Bessie and their 8-year-old son, Dennis. Bessie had married Henry while in her teens but, some eighteen months previously, had begun a friendship with Arthur Franklin who had a cottage about 170yds from her home. Arthur, who was Irish, shared his cottage with his brother, Frank. Over time, Franklin's friendship with Bessie had slowly deepened and he found himself falling in love with her. Eventually, at his instigation, Bessie left her husband and moved in with the two brothers.

According to Arthur Franklin, Henry Nott was bone-idle. When Bessie first moved into Nott's house, she was half-starved and completely worn down with the effort of almost single-handedly running the small poultry farm that provided the sole income for the Nott family. When Franklin first suggested that Bessie leave her husband and move in with him, Nott had apparently been less concerned about losing his wife than about who was going to do all the work when she was gone. Franklin maintained that Nott attempted to negotiate terms with him, stating that if Bessie continued to feed the poultry, look after Dennis and generally help out on the Notts' smallholding, then he would be quite happy for her to go to Franklin at nights.

In the end, Dennis continued to live with his father but was a regular visitor to the Franklin household and remained close to both of his parents, even though they lived apart. However, his father had not yet given up hope that his wife would return to him, even if only for the sake of their son and, on 7 May 1935, his hopes were finally realised when Bessie returned to her marital home. Just two days later, Henry lay severely wounded in Cossham Hospital and his wife was dead.

On 9 May, Mrs Robbins, another resident of the woods, ran down the hill to the home of Priscilla Rose (Dolly) Dyer. She had heard the sound of raised voices followed by gunshots from the Notts' home and she begged Dolly to go and investigate, being reluctant to do so herself as she had her young baby with her. Dolly went over to the Notts and called out for Henry and Bessie, but received no response. Then she spotted Franklin, who was trembling and appeared agitated.

Is anything the matter, Mr Franklin?' she asked.

'Yes,' replied Franklin. 'You had better fetch the police. I have killed Bessie and put a shot into Mr Nott.'

Dolly Dyer bravely walked with Franklin to his own home. On the way they met Dolly's husband and it was he who went for the police and a doctor.

Meanwhile, a severely injured Henry Nott was making good his escape, crawling across a field towards the nearest telephone, blood pouring from his head and shoulder. He was eventually assisted by a coalman delivering to a nearby property. The St John Ambulance was summoned and Nott was taken to hospital, where he was immediately placed under police protection. His condition was said to be critical.

By the time the police arrived, Franklin was sitting quietly on the ground in a clearing in the woods waiting for them. The first officer on the scene, Police Sergeant Auger from Hanham police station, quickly arrested him without any fuss and detained him in his cottage. When Inspector Symons arrived on the scene, he saw the body of a woman – whom he took to be Franklin's wife – lying face down on the ground, her head completely shattered by gunshot fired at close range. Symons promptly charged Franklin with 'feloniously killing and shooting her' and warned him that there might be an additional charge of killing a man.

A post-mortem examination on the body of Mrs Nott, carried out by Dr A.L. Taylor, a pathologist at Bristol General Hospital, showed that she had received horrendous injuries. She had been shot twice, once in the shoulder and once in the head. The shot to the head had quite literally blown her brain completely out of her skull and she had died instantly. Meanwhile, Henry Nott was still being treated in hospital. An X-ray showed more than forty shotgun pellets were embedded in his head and he was so severely wounded that one of his eyes eventually had to be removed.

Franklin appeared before magistrates at Staple Hill Police Court where he was told that he was eligible for legal aid. Having pleaded guilty to the charges against him, Franklin persistently refused all offers of assistance, telling magistrates, 'You need not go to any trouble. I do not want legal aid.'

His trial took place at the Gloucester Assizes on 5 June 1935 before Mr Justice MacNaghten. There it emerged that, on the day of the murder, Bessie Nott had been walking towards her husband's home when Franklin had shot her from behind with his sporting gun, shooting her again after she had fallen to the ground. Witnesses heard Franklin say that he was doing this because she was returning to her husband. He couldn't bear the thought of her leaving him and going back to the man he referred to as 'that black beast'.

Nott, who was working close by, heard his wife scream, followed by the sound of shots. Running to investigate, he saw Franklin standing there with the single-barrelled shotgun raised and heard him threaten: 'And you too, you rat.' Nott ran towards the shed where he kept his own gun, but before he could reach it, Franklin fired again, the shot hitting Nott in the head and destroying his left eye. According to Franklin's statement at the time of the murder, he had intended toying with Nott, much in the way that a cat plays with a mouse. However, fortunately for Nott, Franklin had by then run out of cartridges and was unable to fire any further shots.

In court, Franklin once again denied the chance to be granted legal aid and insisted on pleading guilty to the charges against him, leaving the judge no option but to reach for his black cap and pronounce the only prescribed sentence for murder. Asking Franklin if he had anything to say as to why a sentence of death should not be passed, he received the terse reply, 'Nothing.' Thus, only six minutes after first entering the dock, having spoken only eight words in total, Arthur Henry Franklin, aged 45, stepped down again, to be escorted to Gloucester Prison to await his execution.

In his last weeks, Franklin maintained the same stoical, emotionless demeanour that he had shown ever since the shooting. A Roman Catholic, he was attended by Father Roche of St Peter's Church, Gloucester, his only visitor apart from his brother.

The execution took place at 8 a.m. on 26 June 1935. It was carried out by Thomas Pierrepoint, who was assisted by Robert Wilson. The jurors were taken to see the body, despite the protests of one, Robert Williams, who only reluctantly carried out what was described as his 'civil duty' at the insistence of the prison governor.

A few months after the execution, Frank Franklin approached the police and asked for the return of his brother's shotgun. Since Frank had not been involved in the crime and was thought to be of good character, there was no reason to deny his request. Nobody could have imagined that Frank would use the same gun to commit suicide, choosing to take the weapon to the edge of a water-filled quarry behind the cottage he had shared with his brother and end his life.

Dennis Nott grew up to be a healthy, handsome young man who, after completing his National Service in the army, went to work for a firm of agricultural contractors. When he was 21 years old and busy planning for his imminent marriage, he fell from a ladder while loading hay. The fall broke his neck, killing him instantly.

Henry Nott continued to live in Hanham Woods until Kingswood Council bought the land in the 1960s. He was re-housed in Cadbury Heath and later remarried, outliving his second wife. He died in 1989, aged 84.

[Note: Bessie Nott's full name seems to have been Gladys Bessie Nott. In various contemporary accounts of the murder, she is referred to as Gladys, rather than Bessie. Likewise, Henry Nott was often referred to as Harry. The name of Inspector Symons is also alternatively spelled Simons. Their most frequently used names have been selected for this chapter.]

25

'I THINK MY HUSBAND'S DEAD'

Henleaze, 1942

In the early hours of the morning of 8 December 1942, the St John Ambulance Association received a call from a telephone kiosk asking for an ambulance to be sent to an address in Henleaze. 'I think my husband's dead', said the caller dispassionately. When the ambulance pulled up at the door of the house in Wellington Hill West, some seven minutes later, a woman was standing calmly by the open door.

She explained to the attendant, Mr Giles, that her husband had been taking a bath. She became concerned that he was taking rather a long time and went upstairs to check on him, finding him unconscious with his head submerged beneath the water.

Mr Giles rushed upstairs and found the man – 34-year-old Cecil George Cornock – not in the bathroom as he might have expected, but lying on the floor of a locked bedroom, wrapped in a sheet. Giles immediately began artificial respiration, having first made sure that the police and a doctor were sent for.

When Dr Gordon Fells, the Cornocks' own doctor, arrived at 2 a.m., almost an hour later, he quickly pronounced Cornock dead, even though valiant attempts were still being made by Giles to resuscitate him. Fells believed that death had actually occurred some four hours previously and he noticed that the naked body bore the marks of several injuries.

These injuries were later documented by Dr Allen Fraser, honorary pathologist at Bristol Royal Infirmary, who arrived at the house at 5 a.m. to examine the body. Cecil Cornock had numerous bruises on his head, backs of his shoulders, small of his back, backs of his legs, and on his knees, shins and ankles. Strangest of all were the presence of bruises on the deceased's wrists which, according to Dr Fraser, had occurred as a result of the wrists being bound with rope.

His observations were confirmed by the post-mortem examination, at which it was concluded that the cause of Cornock's death had been drowning. However, several injuries to the top of Cornock's head appeared to have been caused while

115

Wellington Hill West, 2007. (©N. Sly)

he was alive and would have been of sufficient force to stun him. The pathologist suggested that Cornock may have had his hands tied behind his back and that his legs were then tied or even held while he was pulled underwater, his struggles resulting in the extensive bruising.

The first police officers on the scene, PC Buckland and Detective Sergeant Godden checked the bathroom as soon as they arrived. They found the bath empty and dry, although with tiny amounts of grit at the bottom. The bathroom window was closed and the curtains drawn, and the flue of the gas geyser, by which means the bath water was heated, had been broken and was lying on the bathroom floor in two pieces.

Naturally, one of their first actions was to take a statement from Cornock's wife, Rosina Ann, usually known as Ann. She told them that Cecil had been suffering from a cold and decided to take a bath to try and relieve his symptoms. She had run his bath, then been interrupted by a knock on the door. The visitor was a friend, Gilbert Kenneth Bedford – Ken, as he preferred to be called.

Cecil had stayed downstairs long enough to say hallo to the visitor then gone to have his bath, with a promise from Ann that she would make him a hot drink. According to Ann, she had become engrossed in chatting to Ken and some time had passed before she noticed that her husband had not called downstairs for his drink. She had gone up to check on him and found him lying motionless in the bath with his face submerged.

Her first thought, she stated, had been to attempt to take her husband's pulse. Then, she pulled out the bath plug to drain the water, turned off the gas water heater and called to Ken for help.

Ken was disabled with an acute form of arthritis that left his hip joints permanently fixed. He usually walked with the aid of two sticks; hence it is difficult to imagine him racing upstairs to render first aid. Yet he did manage to get upstairs and Ann and Ken then engaged in a prolonged struggle to get the wet – and doubtless slippery – body of Cecil Cornock out of the bath.

Several times the body slipped out of their hands and, in wrestling with it, Ken steadied himself on the geyser flue, which broke. Finally, they had the body precariously balanced on the edge of the bath, at which point it slipped from their grasp once again, the head crashing into the bathroom door.

The two then dragged Cecil's body from the bathroom into the bedroom where, according to Ann, she removed her husband's false teeth and began to give him artificial respiration. However, before long, the strenuous effort proved too much for her and, feeling tired and faint, she paused to drink a cup of tea that Ken had made for her and to take two aspirins.

Next, not wanting to go outside on a cold winter's evening in damp clothes, she had changed her skirt and jumper before going to the telephone box to call for assistance. While waiting for the ambulance to arrive, she had even given the bath a quick clean.

Ken Bedford was also asked to make a statement. He confirmed that he had arrived at the house at about 10.15 p.m. and that, at 11 p.m., Ann had gone to check on her husband and called downstairs for help. Given his disabilities, it would have taken Ken some time to climb the stairs and, when he reached the bathroom, Cecil's head was still submerged and Ann had made no effort either to empty the bath or to raise her husband's head above water. Ken estimated that it had taken about twenty minutes to get Cecil out of the bath, after which they immediately began artificial respiration. Ann had soon felt exhausted by her efforts and the couple then took a further hour to move Cecil from the bathroom to the bedroom. Between helping to remove the body from the bath and dragging it to the bedroom, he had made a cup of tea, which he and Ann had drunk in the lounge.

Bedford later made a second statement. This time he contradicted his original story by stating that artificial respiration had not been given on the bathroom floor, as there was insufficient room. Instead, Ann had only begun her efforts to resuscitate her husband after his body was removed to the bedroom. And the tea had been made and drank only when it became obvious that her efforts were proving fruitless.

The discrepancies in the statements made by the only two witnesses to the incident were enough to arouse suspicion in Detective Superintendent Carter and eventually Ann was forced to amend her statement. She had lied at Ken's request. He had not arrived at 10.15 p.m., but had in fact been at the house all day. He had been unwilling to admit that because, only a few months before Cornock's drowning, he had been involved in yet another sudden death.

In August 1946, he had gone out for the evening with his then girlfriend, 21-year-old Pauline Keeling, who was Ann's niece. On the way home, without any warning, Pauline had suddenly collapsed. She was rushed to hospital but died a few days later of pulmonary oedema, the cause of which was never established. Ken had felt it would look suspicious if he were closely involved in a second sudden death so soon after the first, and Ann had agreed to lie about the timing of his visit in order to protect him.

On the following day, in yet another statement, Ken admitted to the police that he had lied about the time of his arrival because he didn't want people to gain the impression that he was a regular visitor to the house. He also dropped a bombshell by stating that when Cecil was removed from the bath, his wrists were bound behind him. Ann had cut the ropes with scissors and instructed Ken not to mention it because she was afraid that, if the fact that Cecil's hands were tied were revealed, it would make people think that she had murdered her husband.

The fact that Ken seemed to find nothing unusual about Cecil's hands being tied is indicative of the strange relationship that existed between himself, Ann and Cecil.

Ken had first met Ann at the wake for his girlfriend, Pauline, which was held at Ann's parents' home in Northampton Street, Bath. At the time, Ken had been suffering from an ulcerated leg that required regular dressing and, unable to find anyone willing to undertake this task, he had been only too pleased to accept when Ann offered to help. He regularly visited her at home in Bristol, often staying overnight or even for the whole weekend, sometimes sleeping on the sofa, sometimes in the bedroom of Ann and Cecil's 10-year-old son, Maurice.

Cecil Cornock worked as a cost inspector for the Ministry of Aircraft Production and his work often took him away from home. He would frequently take a room in a boarding house near Hyde Park in London. Disturbed by the apparent closeness that was developing between his wife and Bedford, he told his mother that he intended to write to Ken telling him to keep away. Cecil was also planning to move to London permanently, taking his wife and son with him.

It seemed evident that there was some attraction between Ann and Ken. The letters they wrote to each other, discovered torn into pieces at the house in Wellington Hill West after Cecil's death, were couched in terms of affection. One letter from Ken to Ann read: 'Darling, you do make me jealous... I realise more and more that I could not go on without you, my dearest. You belong to me, and that knowledge has given me happiness.' Ann replied in a similar vein: 'There is only one thing I am living for, and that is the day when I can say you are really mine...'

Ann had told Ken that she was not happy in her marriage, accusing Cecil of bullying their son and of keeping her short of money. And she had also confided in Ken about the bizarre sexual practices that she was forced to suffer at the hands of her husband.

Nowadays, Cecil's sexual proclivities seem almost tame. Yet, in the 1940s, his taste for dressing in women's clothes and being tied up and beaten would have been regarded as sickening perversions, which would certainly have given Ann grounds for divorce had she wanted. However, whatever Ann endured in the bedroom was more than compensated for by the financial security that Cecil provided. In the past, Ann had known poverty and had also worked as a domestic servant – servicing Cecil's unusual sexual needs was a small price to pay for the home of her own that she had always craved.

Ken had witnessed Cecil's strange behaviour with his own eyes. On one of his visits to the Cornocks' home, Ann had told him that if he ever heard strange sounds coming from the breakfast room of their house, he should go into the cupboard under the stairs, where a small window afforded a view into the room.

Accordingly, on 6 December, after Maurice had gone to bed, Cecil asked Ann to come into the breakfast room with him for a game of draughts. Ann did as she was asked and before long Ken heard curious noises. He slipped quietly into the cupboard under the stairs and peered through the window where he saw Cecil, a gag in his mouth, dressed in a woman's dress with padding inserted to give the impression of breasts.

Cecil was bound hand and foot, bending over a washing boiler that had been moved into the breakfast room. A reluctant Ann was thrashing him with a cane, while he begged her in a muffled voice, 'Lower'.

Sickened by what he had seen, Ken had been filled with sympathy for Ann, who told him that sometimes Cecil even insisted that the couple went out into the woods, demanding to be tied to a tree and caned.

Hence, Ken would not have been unduly surprised to see Cecil lying naked and bound in the bath – but it is conceivable that he would have agreed to preserve Ann's modesty by neglecting to mention it to the police in his first statement.

The investigating officers were not quite so accommodating. Ann had already mentioned to them that her husband was a 'pervert' who was inclined to become violent if she didn't comply with his sexual demands. She had shown them a suitcase of women's clothes, stockings and underwear that her husband had concealed in the house. Many of the clothes were stained with blood and semen and a similar bag of clothes was later found at Cecil's London rooms.

She also showed them a cane, kept in a cupboard in the scullery, with which she used to beat her husband at his insistence. And finally she admitted that, before Cecil's last bath, she had tied his wrists, but insisted that the rope was removed before he got into the bath. When she was asked to produce the rope, she again went to the scullery cupboard and produced three pieces of white rope from a peg bag. However, when it was pointed out to her that the rope was wet, she maintained that Cecil had accidentally dropped it into in the bath water.

Ann also denied any relationship between herself and Ken other than that she was helping him with his bad leg. While Ken had admitted to kissing and cuddling, she insisted that there had been nothing more intimate between them than a friendly peck on the cheek.

Her explanations didn't ring true to the police and, on 10 December, she was arrested and formally charged with the murder of her husband.

The case came before magistrates in January 1947 and the outcome was that Ann was committed for trial at the Bristol Assizes for the murder of Ceil Cornock. Awaiting her trial in Cardiff Gaol, a routine medical examination in February showed that she was two months' pregnant. Ken Bedford was not charged since it was believed that his crippling disability would have made it physically impossible for him to commit the murder.

Ann Cornock's trial opened at the Bristol Assizes on 4 March 1947 before Mr Justice Croom-Johnson, with G.D. 'Khaki' Roberts KC and Henry Elam prosecuting and J.D. Casswell KC conducting the defence, supported by C.F. Ingle. Ann seemed completely emotionless throughout the proceedings, a trait her defence counsel attributed to years of suppressing her emotions during her strange and loveless marriage.

Crowds attending the trial of Ann Cornock at the Bristol Assizes. (Courtesy of Bristol Central Library Archives)

The police produced the torn up letters found at the Cornocks' home, which they had painstakingly pieced together, using them as evidence of an intimate relationship between Ann and Ken. However, both continued to deny any intimacy whatsoever, with Ken admitting in the witness box that he was actually a virgin and therefore couldn't possibly be the father of Ann's unborn child as the prosecution had suggested.

Dr Fraser gave evidence about the strange marks on Cecil's body and was adamant that the bruises on Cecil's head had been caused by being hit with an object before his death, rather than as a result of his rather clumsy removal from the bath. A wooden toy boat found in the bathroom and thought by police to have been used to strike Cecil was produced in court. Casswell was able to demonstrate that it couldn't have been used as a weapon after an examination by Mr Parks of the Home Office South Western Forensic Science Laboratory showed that it bore absolutely no traces of blood, hair or forensic evidence of any kind.

Casswell then called his own medical witness, Dr Charles Gibson, an experienced police surgeon who worked as an assistant physician in the casualty department at Bath United Royal Hospital. Gibson had carried out an experiment, asking an assistant to tie him up with cotton cord. After fifteen minutes, the cord was removed and Gibson then sat in a hot bath for thirty minutes. He was able to assure the court that the cord marks on his wrist were still evident when he got out of the bath, thus adding credence to Ann's story that the marks remained from a session of consensual bondage before Cecil took his bath. Gibson also supported Ann's statement that the marks on her husband's head could have been caused by it being bumped on the door and, although he couldn't state that the bruises were caused after Cecil's death, he did concede that they were consistent with his head havin been bumped on a flat surface while his heart was still beating feebly.

In addition, Gibson had presented his findings to celebrated pathologist Sir Bernard Spilsbury for a second opinion. Spilsbury's declining health prevented him from travelling to Bristol to give evidence – indeed, he was to commit suicide later that same year – but he questioned the film that had been used by the police to take photographs of the body. When Gibson established that the police had used photographic plates which caused red marks to appear as black, Spilsbury concurred with Gibson's suggestions that the police photographs were showing bruising on the body that simply wasn't there.

This left the two main medical witnesses in opposition and would mean that the outcome of the trial would depend largely on which of the two the jury found the most credible.

Ann Cornock maintained her calm, impassive demeanour as she was called to the witness box, giving her evidence clearly and in a determined manner. Now she stated that Cecil had often fallen asleep in the bath in the past and that he had also recently been experiencing blackouts, a fact he had never mentioned to his doctor. Ann explained the delay between finding her husband's body and summoning assistance by saying that she was distressed and confused and it simply hadn't occurred to her to request help.

She told the court that, while hers was a loveless marriage, she and Cecil had been on friendly terms up to the moment of his death. And, when challenged about the statement she had made in which she asserted that she and Cecil had not had sexual relations for many years, she explained that she had meant that they rarely had intercourse – the last time was about two weeks before her husband's death and had resulted in her pregnancy, something she had been unaware of when making her original statement.

The prosecution made much of the fact that her first reaction on finding her husband was to take his pulse, before even thinking to ensure that his head had been lifted from under the water. Before her marriage, Ann had spent a short time as a probationer nurse, a fact that was obviously very relevant. However, when enquiries were made, there was no trace of her having been employed by a hospital and a mental home where she was supposed to have worked for six months had since closed down and no records had been kept.

Questioned about Ken Bedford, Ann stated that it had never occurred to her to suggest that he go for help while she tried to resuscitate her husband. The telephone kiosk, from which Ann eventually summoned an ambulance, was less than 200yds away from the house and there were also neighbours whom Ken could have approached – instead, Ken seems to have stood idly by or made tea while the drama of Cecil's death was taking place.

Finally, Ann addressed the subject of the love letters between herself and Ken. Again, she vehemently denied any romantic feelings for him, stating that she had written hers as an exercise, just to prove to Ken that she could write a love letter. She was in the habit of writing to her husband while he was away in London and, on one occasion, Ken had looked over her shoulder while she was writing and commented, 'I don't call that much of a love letter'. She had promptly dashed off a few romantic lines to show him that she could produce a tender letter if she wished, then they had laughed about the letter together and she had torn it up.

The defence was able to demonstrate that the torn up letter had not been folded at any time, so had never been inserted into an envelope.

In summing up the case for the defence at the conclusion of the trial, Casswell made much of the apparent disagreement between the two medical experts and suggested that the discrepancies in Ann's various statements to the police could be attributed to shock and exhaustion. The prosecution, meanwhile, tried to convince the jury that a possible motive for the murder of Cecil Cornock was the passion that his wife felt for Ken Bedford.

The prosecution made much of the fact that Ann, now pregnant, had made a statement in which she had denied having a sexual relationship with Cecil. 'Are we not entitled to draw the reasonable conclusion that the love and passion between the two [Ken and Ann] has produced this result?' asked Mr Roberts.

Roberts also tried to explain the delay in calling for assistance for Cecil Cornock. The long interval between finding the body and summoning the ambulance had, he suggested, been used by Ken and Ann to remove, suppress or conceal evidence and to concoct a feasible story.

Finally, it was left to the judge, Croom-Johnson, to address the jury. Defending counsel Casswell wrote in his memoirs, *A Lance for Liberty*, that throughout the trial, he had had the impression that the judge was 'dead against the accused'. Using a plaster model of Cecil Cornock's head, with black patches showing the location of the bruises, Croom-Johnson reminded the jury that Dr Fraser had examined the body soon after death, whereas Dr Gibson had not actually examined the body. This, said the judge, was a case of murder or nothing – there was no room for a verdict of manslaughter. Then, asking the jury to take the model of the plaster head with them in order to best decide whether the injuries were deliberate or accidental, he sent them to begin their deliberations.

It took the jury an hour and a quarter to return a verdict of 'Not Guilty'.

Ann was immediately discharged and, while an ambulance man assisted an emotional Ken Bedford from the court, she quickly left for a secret destination on the south coast. The very next day, Bedford went to the local register office to give notice of a marriage between himself and Ann Cornock. However, it appears that this was done without first consulting his bride-to-be, since the notice was quickly withdrawn. Ann dismissed the idea of marriage as ridiculous, telling reporters that she was not interested in Bedford and that her friendship with him was finished.

Ann eventually returned to Bath, where she gave birth to a daughter in the autumn of 1947. Neither she nor Ken Bedford ever made any further comment about the events on the night of 7 December 1946 that led to the untimely death by drowning of Cecil George Cornock.

26

THE LIGHT THAT FAILED

The film, which was based on a story by Rudyard Kipling, starred Ronald Colman, who played the part of Richard Kelmar. Kelmar is a former British Army Officer, now struggling to make his name as an artist. However, an old war wound threatens his eyesight and, realising that he is slowly going blind, Kelmar chooses to return to the Sudan where he rides into battle one last time, all the while anticipating the bullet that will finally end his life.

As *The Light that Failed* unfolded in the Odeon cinema on 29 May 1946, the rapt audience heard nothing but the sound of gunfire from the film soundtrack. Nobody realised that a very real life and death drama was being played out in the cinema even as they watched the movie, until a message was flashed across the big screen asking if there was a doctor in the house.

Some of the cinema staff heard the gunshot, but assumed it had either been part of the film, a car backfiring outside or a door slamming. One of the doormen, Mr Jackson, did begin to try and locate the source of the loud bang, but it was only when the supervisor of the cinema's restaurant went to ask the manager if he would like a cup of tea that the shooting was discovered. The restaurant supervisor found the manager sprawled on the floor of his office with blood pouring from a wound in his temple. Barely conscious, 33-year-old Robert Parrington Jackson, usually known as Jacko, was groaning and mumbling unintelligibly. The seat of his chair had been knocked out and lay on the office floor, but, other than that, there were no signs of a struggle having taken place.

Jacko was rushed by ambulance to the Bristol Royal Infirmary. Shortly after he left, his wife arrived at the cinema, intending to call on her husband and then watch the evening showing of the film. She was immediately taken to her husband's bedside. A justice of the peace was also hurriedly despatched to the hospital, in the hope that the wounded man would recover sufficiently to give a statement. However, at 3.35 a.m., with his wife at his side, Parrington Jackson died without ever regaining consciousness. He left a 4-year-old son.

123

Zetland Road. (Courtesy of Derek Fisher, Bygone Bristol)

Parrington Jackson, who lived on Zetland Road, had been manager of the Odeon since 1940, although he had recently served for five and a half years as a gunner in the Royal Navy, returning to his position at the cinema only seven weeks prior to his death. He was something of an action man and, before moving to Bristol, had lived in Hollywood, taking small parts in films and working as a radio announcer. He was ideally suited to his job as manager of a cinema, popular with both staff and patrons alike. Always immaculately dressed in a formal evening suit while on duty, he had a talent for organising charity fundraisers at which the stars of the big screen, such as Margaret Lockwood, would be persuaded to make personal appearances.

Police were called to the Odeon cinema by a patron and, as soon as the last filmgoer had left the premises, the doors were locked and interviewing of the staff began. Detectives learned that, shortly before the shooting, Jacko had been laughing and joking with the restaurant staff, having just collected the takings from the box office. The money was later found untouched in his office, the keys to the safe in his jacket pocket.

The investigating officers, headed by Superintendent Fred Carter, initially found themselves with three mysteries to solve. Firstly, what was the motive behind the killing of the popular and affable cinema manager? Secondly, where was the murder weapon? And thirdly, who was the cinema patron who had telephoned them to report the shooting?

The latter riddle was soon solved when, after an appeal from the police, the telephone caller came forward and gave what police described as 'a most helpful statement'. As a result of information given by the caller, a description was issued of a man whom police were seeking to assist with their enquiries. He was seen hanging around in the cinema lounge between 5.30 p.m. and 6 p.m. on the night before the shooting. Staff remembered that, at about 5.45 p.m. on 29 May, a second man had eaten sardines on toast in the cinema restaurant then sat on a sofa in the lounge reading the evening newspapers. He was also asked to come forward so that he might be eliminated from the investigation.

The first man was described as between 30 and 35 years of age, of medium build with a longish face, dark hair and a ruddy complexion. He was clean-shaven and dressed in a well-worn, somewhat shiny, dark suit that was possibly navy blue in colour. He wore a white collar with a dark coloured tie and carried an old mackintosh coat. He had spoken to an usherette, telling her that he was waiting for someone, but had no discernible accent. His one outstanding feature was his lips, which were variously described as 'tight' or 'pursed'.

The second man was in his mid to late twenties, with untidy dark brown hair, blue eyes and decaying teeth. He was also clean-shaven, with a sallow complexion and rather sunken cheeks. He too wore a shiny navy blue suit with a collar and tie, carried a soiled mackintosh and was said to look ill or neglected.

In addition, a blonde woman was seen sitting in a blue saloon car in the Odeon car park at around the time of the attack. The car park attendant, Ernest Thomas, described her as well-dressed and well-spoken but stated that she appeared rather flustered. She had twice left her car and walked in the direction of Union Street.

It was stressed that there was nothing sinister about the three people described but that detectives simply felt that they could hold vital information about the murder. Meanwhile, it was reported in the *Bristol Evening Post* that, in the early hours of the morning after Parrington Jackson's murder, night watchman Harry Knight had surprised an intruder in another Bristol cinema. Mr Knight told police that he had been sitting reading when, at about 1.30 a.m., he heard a bang at the front doors of the New Palace Theatre in Baldwin Street. He initially thought that the noise was being made by a policeman checking the door locks, but, on hearing a further banging noise, he went to investigate and surprised a man standing by the pay box in the cinema vestibule. Knight bravely told the man to 'Clear off!' and, when the intruder showed no signs of obeying, Knight blew his whistle for assistance. At this, the man ran out of the cinema, heading in the direction of Bristol Bridge. Although the police arrived shortly afterwards, the intruder was long gone.

The investigating officers were working on the assumption that the motive for the murder had been robbery and that the killer had made his escape through a roof void, which ran the length of the theatre, leading from a storeroom adjacent to the manager's office to the gallery exit in Union Street. The three or four minute delay in finding Mr Parrington Jackson would have allowed ample time for his killer to have escaped – a theory tested and proven by a young detective who managed to crawl through the roof space in just over a minute. The detective emerged from the roof void dusty, dishevelled and showing obvious signs of physical exertion and police appealed to members of the public for sightings of anyone in this state in the vicinity of the cinema on the evening of the murder.

Detectives subjected the entire cinema to a thorough fingertip search, often working by torchlight as they meticulously combed every nook and cranny. Home Office pathologist Professor J.M. Webster was called in to analyse the dust from the roof void, while a firearms expert was brought from Birmingham to give his opinion on the weapon used.

Central Union Street. (Courtesy of Derek Fisher, Bygone Bristol*)*

Smarts
NEW
PREMISES

Professor Webster later gave evidence at the inquest into Parrington Jackson's death, detailing the nature of his injuries. He described a single gunshot wound to the head, which had resulted in a fractured skull, bleeding and lacerations to the brain. The point of entry of the bullet was 3in above the right eye and it had exited just over the left eye. In Webster's opinion, the shot had been fired from above and behind the victim, passing from right to left. There was no blackening or burning of the surrounding skin and no gunpowder residue, which suggested that the gun hadn't been fired at close range. Webster believed that the weapon used had been a heavy calibre gun, possibly a service revolver. He discounted any suggestion that the wound was self-inflicted.

The police did not confine their search to the inside of the cinema. Every bombsite and air-raid shelter in the city was examined in the hunt for the missing weapon and dozens of people were interviewed, their statements amounting to many thousands of words. A watch was kept at Temple Meads and at other stations in the West Country and docks and ports countrywide were closely monitored. Searches were made at Yeovil and Bridgwater. Cars were stopped in places as far away as Lancashire and Cheshire and their occupants interrogated, and in Cardiff, the entire CID engaged in a search of hotels, guesthouses and hostels. Slides showing detailed descriptions of the people police wished to interview were displayed on the screens of twenty cinemas in Bristol and the surrounding area.

Police inspected the registers of local hotels and boarding houses, on some occasions rousing the occupants from their beds to be questioned. Two young Bristol men, Michael Thomas and Thomas Hewlett, who had hitchhiked to London to see the Victory rehearsal and were staying at the YMCA in Tottenham Court, were woken by detectives at 1.45 a.m. Fortunately, they were quickly able to satisfy the police that they had had no involvement in the murder.

None of the people whose descriptions had been issued by the police ever came forward to be interviewed. However, the manageress of a café in Clifton called the CID to report that a man closely matching the description of 'pursed lips' had called at her establishment at about 5.20 p.m. on the Friday after the murder. Describing the man as seeming in a dazed condition, the witness said that, having been told the café was closed, he wandered away as if he didn't know where he was going. She had seen the man again later that day, walking apparently aimlessly in the rain.

Almost three weeks after the murder, a man said to bear a close resemblance to 'pursed lips' mysteriously disappeared from a house in Clifton. Police managed to trace him and established that he had a legitimate reason for leaving and had no connection with the murder. At the same time, another man of similar appearance was questioned, having been found in a distressed condition in the city centre, but he had been out of the area on the crucial day.

At the end of July, a Colt 45 automatic pistol was found by a workman while cleaning out a small water tank in the vicinity of the cinema and handed to the police. At around this time, US Military Police visited the city after a deserter from the American Forces, who escaped from detention in Dieppe, was seen in Bristol. The officers investigating the murder were also very anxious to speak to this man and military and civil police combined their efforts to find him in a widespread search, which ultimately proved fruitless.

It seemed that no matter how thoroughly the police investigated the case, they were no nearer to discovering the identity of Mr Parrington Jackson's killer. Was robbery the motive for the murder? Did Parrington Jackson disturb an intruder in his office? If this were the case, then it suggests that the perpetrator was someone who was familiar with both the layout and the everyday routines of the cinema.

It suggests a murderer who knew that the manager would have collected the cinema takings – around £300 – and taken them to his office to be placed in the safe. Someone who knew about the roof void and planned to use it as a means of escape. Someone who, perhaps having seen the film, managed to time the fatal shot to coincide with those portrayed on the big screen to lessen the impact of the noise. It also suggests that the murderer was quite a small, agile man, since parts of his escape route through the roof void involved squeezing through a gap that was only 8in wide.

Or was the murder the result of a private quarrel between the cinema manager and an unknown individual? It must be remembered that no money was stolen and the key to the safe was found in Jacko's pocket. It was hinted at the time of the murder that the popular cinema manager was especially popular with women – could the murderer have been a jealous husband or boyfriend with a real or imagined grievance?

Was there any connection between the murder at the Odeon and the intruder at the New Palace Theatre?

Whatever the motive, the case of Robert Parrington Jackson's murder gradually went cold and seemed no nearer to being solved until there was a surprise breakthrough in the 1990s.

A man named Jeff Fisher went to the police saying that his father, Billy 'The Fish' Fisher had made a deathbed confession to the killing. According to Fisher, his father and another petty criminal, known as Duckey Leonard, had travelled from South Wales to Bristol with the sole intention of robbing the Odeon cinema. They had been surprised in the act by Parrington Jackson and had shot him in a state of panic.

Naturally, since Fisher was now dead, police were unable to verify the confession, so officially, the murder of Mr Parrington Jackson remains unsolved to this day.

27

'GERT, ARE YOU THERE?'

Stokes Croft, 1949

At 66 years old, many people are beginning to think about taking life a little easier, but not Gertrude Dorothea O'Leary. Until the death of her sister in 1940, the two women had run The Bell, a busy public house in Hillgrove Street. Now living alone, apart from her beloved cats, Miss O'Leary had established her own very successful business, an off-licence in Thomas Street. As well as her business activities, she was a practicing Roman Catholic and a regular worshipper at St Mary's Church on The Quay where she often played the piano for social gatherings. Described as a very popular lady, she was well liked by all the neighbours and was known as an extremely kind person, who donated generously to animal charities.

On 30 June 1949, residents from Dalton Square had gone on their annual outing – a day trip to Weston-super-Mare. Hence the area was unusually quiet when, at about 10.30 a.m., Mrs Metcalfe looked out of her front window and noticed her elderly neighbour, Mrs Brown, in conversation with a disreputable looking man. Thinking that Mrs Brown looked nervous, Mrs Metcalfe shouted from her window to see what the man wanted. He replied that he was looking for lodgings and, on being told that there were none in the area, walked off, heading in the direction of Stokes Croft. Mrs Metcalfe thought no more about the chance encounter until that evening, when a terrible discovery was made at Gertrude O'Leary's premises.

It had been a long, hot day and Fred Dibble, a neighbour of Miss O'Leary, was looking forward to a few thirst-quenching bottles of beer. Miss O'Leary usually closed the off-licence in the afternoons and reopened in the evenings, but on this particular evening, her regular opening time came and went with no sign of any activity at the shop. Dibble noticed that the door to the off-licence yard was open, something which struck him as odd, since it was normally only opened on Fridays to allow the ash men access. Concerned, he went for a closer look and it was then that he noticed that the door leading from the yard into the living quarters was also open.

Right: *Thomas Street. (Courtesy of Derek Fisher, Bygone Bristol)*

Below: *Stokes Croft, early 1900s. (Author's collection)*

Dibble popped his head around the kitchen door and called, 'Gert, are you there?' Receiving no response, he realised that there was something seriously amiss and immediately called the police.

When the police arrived, they went into the living room behind the shop where they found Miss O'Leary stretched out on the floor. She had been hit over the head with a beer flagon, causing severe wounds, and had also been strangled with a cord – a post-mortem examination later revealed that she had died from shock as a result of her injuries. The room had been ransacked, drawers tipped out and papers were scattered all around Miss O'Leary's body. The police later described the scene as 'a shambles'.

It was established that a number of items were missing from the premises, particularly a 9ct gold ladies wristwatch with a white enamelled dial and a 9ct gold pendant studded with amethysts and seed pearls, with a large amethyst drop.

As soon as the body was discovered, a large contingent of CID men was mobilised under the lead of Detective Superintendent Phillips, who had been promoted from Chief Inspector only hours before the murder. As well as making a close search of the off-licence and living quarters, the detectives initiated house-to-house enquiries in the immediate area, which elicited several new clues.

The first of these came from Mrs Elizabeth Sealey, a near neighbour, who had been in her backyard at around 3 p.m. on the afternoon of Miss O'Leary's killing. She described hearing a stifled scream and, shortly afterwards, saw a man wearing a trilby hat leaving the rear of the off-licence and walking across open land nearby.

It seemed that the last person to see Miss O'Leary alive, apart from her killer, was Mrs Mabel Long, who had visited her at about 2.30 p.m. on the afternoon of the murder. Mrs Long reported that Gertrude had been on the point of closing the off-licence for the afternoon and was perfectly well, if feeling a little tired. Local residents had noticed that the door between the shop and Miss O'Leary's living quarters had been closed throughout most of the afternoon, which was unusual. It was Miss O'Leary's habit to leave the door open at all times to allow her cats to wander in and out at will.

And then, of course, there was the mysterious stranger asking for accommodation in the vicinity. When interviewed, Mrs Metcalfe described the stranger as being about 45 years old and about 5ft 3in tall, of slim build. He was wearing a dirty mackintosh, old grey trousers, an old-looking trilby hat and down-at-heel shoes. Mrs Metcalfe had actually seen the same man in the area a couple of days earlier and she recalled that he had then been carrying a parcel. When she spoke to him on the morning of the murder he had seemed well spoken but did not have an identifiable accent.

Indeed, the entire neighbourhood seemed to have been bristling with suspicious strangers. Two people living near the off-licence reported seeing a stranger – possibly the same man – close to the premises on the afternoon of the murder. Another local resident, Miss Pat Fowler of Dalton Square, had seen a strange man being served in Miss O'Leary's shop a few days before. When the man left, Miss O'Leary had seemed nervous and had told Miss Fowler that the man had been in the shop before and that she 'didn't like the look of him'. This man was also shabbily dressed and described as having a swarthy complexion. Another man – again, possibly the same man – had called at the shop some time previously and Miss O'Leary had told her friends about him, saying that she had had difficulty in getting rid of him. Police also noted that Miss O'Leary's shop had recently been burgled and that a watch had been stolen. The watch that was now missing from the premises was new, bought to replace the stolen one.

Bristol police sought the aid of Scotland Yard in solving the murder and two officers, Detective Superintendent Frank Long and Detective Sergeant Peter Gill, arrived by train to assist with enquiries. By now, the investigating officers had two new leads. A search of a workingmen's boarding house nearby turned up a pair of flannel trousers and a shirt, both of which were bloodstained. It is not recorded whether their owner was traced and was able to give an innocent explanation for the condition of the garments, or whether his identity was ever established, but in either case, the discovery of the clothes brought police no nearer to finding the identity of the killer.

The same was true for the man drinking tea in a café at Highbridge, near Burnham-on-Sea, who was said to have been discussing the murder in some detail less than eight hours after it had been committed and before it had been reported in the newspapers. The man had told other customers that he had been outside Miss O'Leary's premises when the murder had taken place. Despite intensive enquiries, police were never able to trace this gentleman who, if his story were true, would at the very least have been a valuable witness.

Was the killer a local man who specifically chose the day of the outing to Weston-super-Mare to commit the murder, when the area would be deserted and there would have been less of a chance of him being seen? Had he watched Miss O'Leary over a period of time and familiarised himself with her daily routines? Or was the murder an opportunistic attack by a passing stranger who was down on his luck and just happened to come across Miss O'Leary and see the elderly, defenceless lady as an easy target? Ironically, Miss O'Leary's devotion to her cats may have played a part in her murder. One of her favourite kittens had recently disappeared and neighbours believed that she might have neglected to close her doors so that it could get back into the house if it returned.

Several months later, police made an arrest in connection with Miss O'Leary's murder, travelling to Devon to interview a waiter. The suspect was eventually released, having been able to prove that he was working in a Torquay hotel at the time of the killing. He later sued the police for wrongful arrest and was awarded £50 in damages.

The case of the murder of Miss Gertrude O'Leary eventually went cold and although it remains open, it is unsolved to this day.

28

'YOU'RE IN A BIT OF A HURRY, AREN'T YOU?'

Knowle, 1949 and Westbury Park, 1950

On 7 January 1949, it was not quite business as usual at the Knowle branch of Lloyds Bank, on the corner of Broad Walk and Wells Road. The bank was staffed by senior cashier George Barron Black, aged 50, assisted by Donald Twitt, aged 17. It being a Friday, the bank was busy, but one customer seemed to be in no particular hurry.

A bespectacled, well-dressed young man had entered the bank at around 2 p.m. and told Black that he was waiting to meet a bookmaker called Murray. As customers came into the bank throughout the afternoon to conduct their business, two of them actually asked the young man if he was waiting to be served, but on both occasions he politely explained that he was waiting for someone.

Having left the bank briefly once, but returning almost immediately, the young man was still patiently waiting when John Rowe, a trainer at the Knowle greyhound stadium, came into the bank at around 3 p.m. Something about the man's manner aroused Rowe's suspicions and, when he left the bank, he went only as far as the nearest telephone box where he dialled 999 and told the operator, 'There is something queer happening at Lloyds Bank at the junction of Wells Road and Broad Walk.'

Having left his message, timed at 3.09 p.m., Rowe headed back towards the bank, where he spotted the young man leaving. 'You're in a bit of a hurry, aren't you?' Rowe asked the man, who replied that he had just collected a debt. 'You'd better wait a minute', said Rowe, as the man climbed into his car, then he reeled back as the young man suddenly punched him full in the face.

Rowe had been holding onto the car door in an effort to prevent the man from leaving. Now the driver pulled away from the kerb, the open car door swinging closed as he did so, hitting Rowe hard on the head.

Although dazed, Rowe managed to memorise the car number plate and to stagger back to the phone box, where he telephoned the police a second time. 'A rough looking man has just rushed out of the bank and driven towards the city in an Austin 16 car JHY 812.'

134

Broad Walk, Knowle. (Courtesy of Derek Fisher, Bygone Bristol)

Corner of Broad Walk and Wells Road, 2007. (©N. Sly)

An Austin 16 – as used by the Lloyds Bank murderer. (Courtesy of John Jones, J & M Classic Cars)

Police went immediately to the bank where they found that Twitt, the son of a former police inspector, had been shut in a cloakroom. George Black was dead, a bullet wound from a 0.32 calibre gun in his chest, just below the right breast.

Police quickly traced the car described by Mr Rowe. Its owner, Mr F. Chappell, had reported it stolen that very morning. Chappell, the manager of Yeo Bros & Paull, located on the corner of Temple Way and Victoria Street, had parked his car on a bombsite opposite his place of work. Noticing another car parked in its place mid-morning, he had telephoned the police at 11.15 a.m. to report it missing.

One of the company's sales staff, Mr King, was convinced that he had seen his boss's car driving past the building at around lunchtime, the driver tucked in closely behind a van so that his number plate wasn't readily visible. King had immediately dialled 999 and reported the sighting.

The car was seen on two more occasions that afternoon, once at Bedminster shortly after 1 p.m. then again outside a shop near to the bank at around 2 p.m. The first witness noted that the male driver seemed to be having difficulties handling the car and believed that he might have been accompanied by a woman. The second witness was an acquaintance of Mr Chappell, the car's owner. This witness recognised the car but assumed that the male driver he observed was a member of Chappell's staff. The car was found abandoned in Totterdown at about 3.45 p.m. There was no trace of its driver.

Back at the bank, police were conducting a thorough search of the premises. At first it was believed that around £800 had been taken, but when bank officials were allowed back into the premises a few days later, they were able to confirm that the actual sum missing was £1,444 10s. The bank offered a reward of £1,000 for information leading to the arrest of the gunman.

Meanwhile, police issued a description of the killer, based on the statements of Twitt, Rowe and other customers who had visited the bank that day. He was described as aged in his mid-twenties, approximately 5ft 6in tall and of small build, with a pale, round face. He was wearing a dark coat over striped flannel trousers, with a trilby hat and carried a black leather briefcase. He also wore spectacles, although the police were quick to point out that these may have been part of a disguise.

Two women came forward to say that they had heard shots and had seen the robber leaving the bank, walking 'smartly', and witnessed his subsequent struggle with John Rowe. They described him as being very pale and looking shaken.

Several customers had seen the man apparently writing something while in the bank and a scrawled note was found discarded on the floor. It read, 'See you Monday at 2. Missed you today. Joe. Waited until 3 p.m.' Police considered the possibility that the handwriting had been disguised, but eventually released the note to the press in the hope that someone might recognise the writing. They also consulted with a handwriting expert from London, who initially declined to comment on what she called 'so poor a specimen'. Later, having given the handwriting further consideration, she eventually agreed to create a 'profile' of the writer.

With the warning that the writer would not be using his normal pen nib and would also be under stress, she described him as 'a person with a grudge against life, capable of bursts of violence, which are almost dissociated from his normal personality.' She believed that he would show extreme irritation towards the objects of his resentment, relieving his irritations by continual 'pinpricks' against whatever was annoying him, until he had a burst of violence, after which he would be calm again. The writer would be difficult to live with, she suggested, since he was jealous, suspicious, cruel and sneering. He had a poor mentality, no logic, no consecutive thinking and would be a bad worker, who exhibited a mixture of boastfulness and suspicious reserve.

Over the next few weeks, the police followed up numerous leads throughout the country and even abroad. They consulted gunsmiths, asking them to check their records for sales of what was believed to be a 0.32 civilian revolver used in the shooting. They issued 10,000 leaflets and distributed hundreds of copies of the discarded note found at the bank They took the fingerprints of every customer who was known to have visited the bank on the day of the murder, around 200 people in total, which were then compared to those taken from the steering wheel of the getaway vehicle. No matches were found.

An Irish bank robber, who bore a strong resemblance to the Knowle robber, was traced and eliminated by the Irish Garda. Known gang hideouts in London were raided and a watch was placed at all London railway terminals. Taxi drivers were questioned, particularly one who reported driving a man and woman to a Bristol boarding house on the night before the murder. The male passenger bore a strong resemblance to the suspect, while the woman was dressed like a Land Army girl.

A lorry driver came forward to say that he had given a hitchhiker a lift to Wrexham ten days after the shooting and that the man's appearance closely matched the description of the bespectacled gunman. Police at Wrexham confirmed that they had received reports of a man in the area resembling the killer, but he was never traced. Similarly, staff at Yate station were interviewed about a man seen boarding the Gloucester train on the afternoon of 7 January.

Another man went voluntarily to Caerphilly police station to give a statement. He too was very similar in appearance to the robber and had actually been in Bristol at the time of the murder. Police were able to eliminate him from their enquiries.

Then, at the beginning of February, an anonymous letter was sent to the *Bristol Evening Post*. The paper's editor passed it straight to Detective Chief Inspector Melbourne Phillips, who was in charge of the case.

Written in pencil on pale blue writing paper, the note, which had been posted at a town near Bristol, was signed 'X29'. Although the police obviously concealed some of the more specific details contained in the letter, they released an abbreviated version to the press. It read:

> Dear Sir,
> Trace up 'Blonde Lady' who went to_______ taking with her _______ June last. Large car, said her husband was a Detective before coming to _______. Swanked he always kept a gun about the house – sometimes took it out with him.
> Gave address somewhere _______. Woman was very tall and nice to speak to, in August this woman was seen on the terrace of the bowling green club with man in horn-rimmed spectacles, answers the wanted man in every way walking with ______.

The letter went on to suggest a connection between the Knowle bank robbery and the murder of Odeon cinema manager Robert Parrington Jackson three years previously. After the cryptic signature, the writer had added a postscript: 'Address and name of Blonde can no doubt be got from _______ man older than issued – 40 or 50 [sic].'

The identities of 'Blonde' and her husband remain a mystery, since they do not appear to have been traced by the police.

Devon and Cornwall Police became involved when a Bodmin shopkeeper reported that a man bearing a likeness to the suspect had passed a cheque on which the writing resembled that of the note. However, close comparison of the cheque and the note showed no real similarities. Detectives eventually travelled as far as Italy to interview suspects and even took fingerprints from a British man who was part of a gang who had committed a similar robbery in Germany.

In September of the same year, a bank manager was shot dead in the course of an armed robbery at the Midland Bank near Penrith. The killer escaped in a taxi, having apparently killed the taxi driver before carrying out the bank raid. The robber, Charles Corbett Kennedy, subsequently shot himself. Twitt, Rowe and a third witness from the Knowle robbery were taken to view the body at Cumberland. They were unable to identify the dead gunman as the man who had shot and killed George Black.

In spite of their best efforts, the police they were unable to obtain any concrete evidence about the Lloyds Bank gunman. Even when notes stolen in the robbery began to circulate in various parts of the country, it seemed that they were no nearer to identifying the perpetrator.

From the outset, the behaviour of the Lloyds Bank gunman had been strange. He had stolen a car on the morning of the robbery then apparently risked driving it around the busy city until the afternoon. He spent an unprecedented amount of time in the bank, almost inviting potential witnesses to look at him. He wrote and left behind a note – although that could, of course, have been a red herring, deliberately planted to lead investigators astray. He left fingerprints on the getaway vehicle, which suggests that he did not have a prior criminal record. He was cool and confident throughout – and he got away with murder!

Just over a year later, on 13 March 1950, bus conductor Dennis Pullen was collecting fares on the number 28 bus as it turned into North View, when two men hurriedly jumped on board and ran upstairs. 'Fares, please', Pullen called after them.

'In a minute' replied one of the two men in a foreign accent.

Bus driver Jack Martin soon became aware of a commotion outside and spotted a man running alongside the vehicle shouting, 'Stop, there are bandits on your bus!' Martin slammed on the brakes. The two men ran back downstairs and jumped off the bus, running towards Westbury Park in the direction of Redland Green, with a number of people in hot pursuit.

One of the pursuers was 30-year-old Robert Taylor, who worked at the *Evening World* newspaper. Taylor, a keep fit fanatic and martial arts expert, was rapidly gaining on the two men and was about to tackle them when one of the pair turned and fired a revolver, shooting him in the head at point blank range.

An ambulance was called and Taylor was rushed to hospital, but he later died from his injuries.

Meanwhile, a local businessman had already dialled 999, having realised that a raid had taken place at Lloyds Bank on the corner of North View. The police were soon combing the area and the two fleeing men were quickly apprehended.

They were identified as Roman Redel and Zbigniew Gower, Polish nationals, who were both aged 23. The young men had shared a room in City Road, St Paul's, although a year earlier Redel had moved out, having married a 17-year-old cinema usherette, who was also Polish. Both men had, until recently, worked as labourers at the British Oil and Cake Mills at Avonmouth, but had handed in their notice only the week before.

The men had ridden past the bank on the top deck of a bus a few days prior to the robbery. The small branch, with its rather elderly security guard, must have looked an easy target. They had spent a week making vague plans to rob the bank, but had got no further than conducting a quick survey of the general area and deciding that a motorbike would make a good getaway vehicle. (The fact that they didn't possess a motorcycle didn't seem to figure in their plans.) On the morning of the bank robbery, fuelled with gin and beer for Dutch courage, the inept raiders disguised themselves with hats and glasses and caught the bus to Westbury Park, arriving at Lloyds Bank just after 11 a.m.

There were two staff on duty at the time. Ronald Wall, the cashier, had just gone into the manager's office for his morning tea, leaving security guard John Bullock standing in the bank. The two raiders pointed a revolver at Bullock with the words 'This is a hold-up.'

Gesturing with the gun, Redel ordered Bullock into the manager's office. Just as he was about to enter, Wall emerged to see what was happening and was ordered to return. Redel stood in the doorway, his gun pointed at the men inside, while Gower climbed over the bank counter and began to rifle through drawers. The two men then backed out of the building, keeping the gun trained on the bank staff and boarded the bus which conveniently arrived just as they exited the bank. As they left the building, Bullock and Wall were already hot on their heels – it was actually Bullock who shouted at the bus driver to stop.

Redel and Gower were tried for the murder of Robert Taylor before Mr Justice Oliver at the Salisbury Assizes. It was thought that they would not receive an impartial trial at Bristol, since the feelings of the local citizens against them were running high.

The court proceedings went ahead, even though the bank security guard, John Bullock, had received an anonymous threatening letter. Written in block capitals, it read:

YOU AND WALL WILL GET YOUR DESERTS [*sic*] IF OUR TWO BOYS HANG. WE ARE GIVING YOU FAIR WARNING SO AS TO GIVE YOU PLENTY OF TIME TO WISH ALL YOUR RELATIVES GOODBYE.

Both men pleaded 'Not Guilty' to the murder of Robert Taylor, with Redel offering the excuse that the gun went off by accident. He maintained that, if it had been his intention to shoot anyone, then he would have shot the bank staff, thus allowing the two men to escape without being pursued.

The jury took no notice of this explanation, finding both men guilty, although they recommended mercy for Gower on the grounds that he had neither carried nor discharged a gun. The robbers appealed, but to no avail. They were both executed at Winchetser Gaol on 7 July 1960. Albert Pierrepoint carried out the double execution, assisted by Harry Kirk, Harry Allen and Syd Dernley.

Robert Taylor was posthumously awarded a George Cross for his bravery in attempting to foil the two robbers, whose total haul from the raid was the meagre sum of £28.

29

'A MAD IMPULSE CAME OVER ME TO DO IT'

Horfield, 1950

Since the death of her husband, Ethel Merinda Worth, aged 65, barely left the house in Hughenden Road that she shared with her 40-year-old son, Frederick. She had lived in the neighbourhood all her life and felt safe and comfortable there.

Wednesday 20 September 1950 seemed just like any other day to Ethel and Frederick. He went off to work at the Bristol Aeroplane Company (BAC) at Filton; she pottered around the house until Fred arrived home at 1.15 p.m. for his lunch.

Ethel usually took an afternoon nap in her favourite armchair. When Fred returned to work, she settled down in front of the fire, a glass of water ready on the mantelpiece for when she awoke.

Fred arrived home again at 5.30 p.m., shouting a greeting to his mother as he always did when he entered the house. This time, he received no reply. Puzzled, he went into the living room and was shocked to see his mother slumped in her chair, her face covered by a coat. His first thought was that she had suffered a stroke, but when he removed the coat from her face, he could see that she had been beaten. He immediately telephoned Dr Courtney, the family doctor, who in turn rang the police.

The police arrived to find that Ethel had been hit over the head and then strangled. The walls around her chair, and the chair itself were heavily spattered with blood. They immediately began house-to-house enquiries in the neighbourhood, beginning with the Worths' next-door neighbours, Harold and Lilian Woodfield.

The Woodfields were brother and sister and they had another brother, Edward, who lived in nearby Southmead Road with his wife. Edward – usually known as

141

Hughenden Road, 2007. (©N. Sly)

Ted – had known Mrs Worth and had often borrowed small amounts of money from her. Thus he was quite high on the list of people to be interviewed and the very next morning he found Detective Sergeant George Cox on his doorstep.

Told of the murder, Ted's first words were, 'Oh, I'm sorry. That is the first I've heard about it.' However, he agreed to accompany Cox to the police station, where he was interviewed by Superintendent Melbourne Phillips. Asked what he had done on the previous day, Woodfield replied that he had spent the afternoon in bed. Phillips cautioned him to be careful, reminding him that Hughenden Road was only a small place with very few houses and, if he had been anywhere near there in the afternoon, then there was a good likelihood that someone would have seen him.

At this, Woodfield broke into loud sobs, burying his head in his hands. After a few minutes he looked up. 'A mad impulse came over me to do it', he wept. 'I will tell you everything.'

The previous day had been a bad one for Ted Woodfield. Like Fred Worth, he too had worked for BAC, but had suffered a bad case of work-related dermatitis that had left his face covered with an angry red rash. To try and alleviate the problem, the company had transferred him to another department, but Ted had been worried that the rash looked like the outward manifestations of venereal disease and believed that other workers were making fun of him. In despair, he had handed in his notice in July 1950 but, by September, he was feeling the loss of a regular wage packet and had written to his former employers asking them for his old job back.

The company – who actually thought very highly of Woodfield – wrote back, their reply arriving on the morning of 20 September. The letter politely explained that they had no suitable vacancies at the moment, but promised that they would notify him as soon as they had a position available.

Ted's reaction on reading the letter was to crumple it in his hand and throw it across the room, much to the surprise of his wife, Katherine, who, in thirty years, had never seen him react so violently to anything before.

Strangely disturbed by her husband's uncharacteristic behaviour, Katherine left him looking 'very dejected' and went off to work herself. Once she had gone, Ted paid a visit to the Labour Exchange, calling at a pub on his way home for a couple of pints of cider. Having made himself some lunch, it occurred to him to visit Mrs Worth and try to borrow some more money from her, even though he already owed her £1.

He picked up a heavy lemonade bottle and put it into his jacket pocket, then walked to Mrs Worth's house and knocked on the door. As the old lady came to answer his knock, he put his hand into his inside jacket pocket as if reaching for his wallet, intending to give her the impression that the purpose of his visit was to repay the loan. Ethel invited him into the house and, as he followed her along the hallway, his 'mad impulse' came over him and he hit her over the head with the bottle.

Stunned, Mrs Worth made her way back to her chair, where Ted hit her again. He told police that he didn't think that they were hard blows and they were certainly not hard enough to render Mrs Worth unconscious because she apparently begged, 'Don't Ted'. Yet Ted had gone too far. Frightened that the elderly lady would report him, he took a pair of gloves from his pocket and squeezed her throat tightly until she could speak no more.

Once Ethel Worth had been silenced, Ted searched the house, taking a gold watch, a pair of field glasses and all the money from her handbag. He left, walking across Horfield Common, disposing of the bottle and gloves on his way. On arriving home, he made himself a cup of tea before placing the watch in a cigarette case and burying it, with the field glasses, in the earth by his back door. He then made supper for his wife.

That night he was unable to settle at home, eventually taking Katherine out to the Beehive pub on Wellington Hill West and using Mrs Worth's money to buy drinks.

Following Woodfield's full confession, his trial opened at the Bristol Assizes on 22 November 1950 before Mr Justice Devlin. J.D. Casswell defended and did his utmost to convince the jury that Woodfield was insane at the time of the murder.

Describing Woodfield as 'bemused', Casswell did not call him to the stand, but instead produced numerous witnesses who testified to the fact that he was normally the gentlest and mildest of men who never lost his temper. He also had a phobia about the sight of blood, so much so that the sight of a car accident caused him to become very upset.

Woodfield had a family history of mental instability. Both his grandmother and his aunt had been inmates at Gloucester Asylum and his mother was known to be delusional. About three years before the murder, Woodfield himself had been ill. He had bent over and experienced what he described as a 'click in his head', which left him with double vision for some time afterwards. Examined by doctors, Woodfield was diagnosed as having hardened arteries and a blood clot on the brain.

The benchmark for determining insanity is known as the McNaghten Rules and was established after the trial of Daniel McNaghten in 1843 for the murder of

Mr Edward Drummond. McNaghten was suffering from delusions of persecution at the time of the murder and, as a result of his trial and subsequent acquittal, it was established that, for a defence on the grounds of insanity to be successful, it must be clearly proved that at the time of committing the act, the accused was labouring under such a defect of reason, from disease of the mind, as not to know the nature and quality of the act he was doing, or, if he did know it, that he did not know what he was doing was wrong.

Doctors who gave evidence at Woodfield's trial had conflicting opinions about the defendant's mental health and none was prepared to go as far as stating that his condition brought him within the McNaghten rules. Dr Charles Gibson, for the defence, would only concede that Woodfield had some mental abnormality, which might make him liable to resort to violence if he were under great stress. Dr Hodge, who appeared for the prosecution, was not even willing to go this far, stating that while the defendant might be more vulnerable to stress than the average person, he was certainly fully capable of understanding the nature and quality of his actions and the consequences that would inevitably follow.

In his summing up of the case for the jury, Casswell maintained that Woodfield's 'mad impulse', so completely out of character for the normally peaceable, mild-mannered defendant, was sufficient evidence of diminished responsibility and an indication that he was not in his right mind when he killed Mrs Worth. Casswell felt that while Woodfield knew exactly what he was doing and that what he was doing was wrong, he was still unable to refrain from doing it because of mental abnormality.

Unsurprisingly, in view of the conflicting medical evidence they had heard, the jury chose to ignore any question of insanity. Woodfield had taken the lemonade bottle with him when he went to see Mrs Worth, which was seen as evidence of premeditation. And, the fact that he had thrown away the bottle and gloves after killing Mrs Worth and also hidden the spoils from the robbery, such actions were indicative of concealment to avoid detection, suggesting that he was well aware of the likely consequences of his actions.

It took the jury almost three hours to return a verdict, but that verdict was 'Guilty', rather than 'Guilty, but insane.'

Today, the crime may well have been reduced to manslaughter on the grounds of Woodfield's diminished responsibility, but in 1950 there were no grounds for appeal and Edward Isaac Woodfield, aged 49, was executed at Bristol on 14 December 1950.

30

'THIS IS MURDER'

Stapleton, 1957

On Thursday 20 June 1957, Bristol was in the grip of a heat wave. As the weather gradually cooled in the late afternoon, 5-year-old Royston Sheasby, who lived in Brockworth Crescent in Stapleton, began to pester his older sister June to go for a walk. June, who was two years older, was not keen, but Royston was insistent – he wanted to visit a nearby field to see the horses there.

Having told their mother, Barbara, of their intentions, the two children set off hand in hand to the horse pasture. Barbara was engrossed in decorating and, when she next noticed the time, she was horrified to see that it was almost seven o'clock. Knowing that the two children should have been home by then, she immediately raised the alarm.

The disappearance of Royston and June Sheasby sparked one of the biggest searches ever known in England. Thousands of members of the public turned out to help the police comb the area. They painstakingly examined woodland, scrub and grassland around Stapleton, while firemen were called to lower the water in the 60ft-deep Duchess Pond so that divers could trawl its depths. Police dogs criss-crossed the countryside, streams and rivers were waded through, outbuildings were entered and searched, but there were no clues to the whereabouts of the missing children to be found.

Within days of the children's disappearance, a letter was sent to the editors of two Bristol evening papers saying that they were alive and well and demanding the sum of £200 for their safe return. The letter, signed 'West Indians', read:

The children, June and Royston, are alive and well at the moment. It is useless for police to continue searching. We hope they enjoy their bath in the river. My brother and I took the children away Thursday night and they will be returned unhurt on payment of £200. This must be left at G.P.O. addressed to ———, to be called for on Wednesday afternoon. My brother will collect, but if he should be detained I shall kill the children after two hours from time he leaves here. If he is allowed to leave, children will be returned unhurt.

145

Brockworth Crescent, Stapleton. (©N. Sly)

At a press conference, Chief Superintendent M. Phillips, the head of Bristol CID, dismissed the letters as 'a wicked and cruel hoax', stating that charges would be pressed should the writer be traced.

Meanwhile, the search for the missing children went on, hampered by the heavy rain that followed the breaking of the heat wave. Exhausted police officers ignored their days off and turned down overtime pay to continue scouring the countryside for the pair – sadly, the search wasn't to have a happy ending.

At about 9 p.m. on 1 July, PC Brough noticed a tiny hand protruding from the earth in dense undergrowth close to the river Frome as it flowed through Snuff Mills Park. It was Royston Sheasby's hand. Immediately, hundreds of police officers were deployed to the area to search for his sister by torchlight. However, when Royston's body was removed from its shallow grave, under the direction of Dr A.C. Hunt, the pathologist attached to the Home Office Forensic Science Laboratory at Bristol, it quickly became evident that June's body had also been concealed in the same place.

Royston's body was taken to a nearby mortuary, while that of his sister was left under police guard until first light. At a press conference held early on the morning of 2 July, Phillips announced: 'This is murder.' He added that Royston appeared to have injuries to his head, but that no investigation had yet been conducted on June's body. He appealed for information from the public about anyone seen to be acting suspiciously in the area on 20 June.

A later post-mortem examination of the two bodies showed that both children had suffered severe head injuries, probably inflicted with a blunt instrument, which had caused skull fractures. There was no evidence of any sexual assault on either child and no immediately apparent motive for their murders.

Duchess Pond, Stapleton. (Courtesy of Derek Fisher, Bygone Bristol)

Police once again appealed for witnesses, asking specifically for information about a man in a blue striped suit who had been spotted sitting on a log near to the burial site at around the time when the children disappeared.

Exhaustive enquiries were made at four mental hospitals in the immediate vicinity. One patient had failed to return after parole to the nearby Bristol Mental Hospital, but since he had no record of violence and had failed to return from leave on previous occasions, he wasn't considered a particularly high priority for the investigating team.

The police then issued a detailed description of George Weston, a patient who had escaped from Purdown Mental Institution. He was quickly traced and eliminated from their enquiries, but they renewed their appeal in the press for the identity of the man in the blue suit. They also asked for help in tracing a girl, aged about 13, who had been seen with two children at about 7 p.m. on 20 June and two boys who had been fishing on the river bank between about 6 p.m. and 9.30 p.m.

Meanwhile, a number of items of the children's clothing were submitted to the Forensic Science Laboratory for testing and, on 5 July, the police announced enigmatically that not all of the tests had proved negative.

Two days later, it was announced that officers were focusing their attention on the patients of one mental hospital and also on those local residents who had previously been convicted of offences against children. The proximity of so many mental hospitals caused problems for the investigating team as they had received numerous false confessions from patients – it was essential that they eliminated every one of these before continuing with their enquiries. They had still been unsuccessful in tracing 'blue suit'.

Snuff Mills – where the bodies of Royston and June Sheasby were discovered. (Author's collection)

The case took a promising turn during the weekend of 6–7 July. Firstly, the police received an anonymous letter. Handwritten on pale blue notepaper and placed in a white envelope, the letter numbered less than twenty words in total, but was said by police to contain vital information. The writer had apparently seen something that confirmed a suspicion already held by the police. Then, a blue suit was recovered from a storeroom at the Bristol Mental Hospital. It was sent for forensic testing, while the police concentrated on the 146 patients at the hospital who were normally subject to parole. One patient in particular was of great interest and was interviewed several times. His parole was cancelled and he was confined to a special ward under the 24-hour guard of male nurses.

By 11 July, police announced that the writer of the letter, a woman, had come forward. They revealed that the information she had given them was 'useful' and, as a result, they expected to interview a man who had since left Bristol. They also issued a description of a 67-year-old man from Newport, Monmouthshire, who they urgently wanted to trace, as he had been missing from home since the night on which the children's bodies were discovered. Both men were later eliminated from enquiries.

Despite exhaustive police efforts, during which they interviewed more than 25,000 people and took over 2,000 statements, the killer was not apprehended. Although the police continued with their investigation, as time went by, it seemed that they were no nearer to finding the perpetrator of the double murder and the case of the 'babes in the wood', while remaining open, grew cold.

Then, in 1964, there was a sensational new development. Dr A. Hyatt Williams, a consultant psychiatrist, claimed at the International Congress of Psychotherapy in London that a prison inmate who had recently 'died of conscience' had confessed to him that he had killed a young boy and a girl. The inmate, imprisoned for a minor offence, had spoken to the doctor in his capacity as a visiting prison psychiatrist.

The doctor had battled with his own conscience before deciding to reveal the information, although he refused to name the individual concerned, likening himself to a priest who had received confidential evidence in the confessional.

The police went straight to the Home Office who distanced themselves from the controversy, stating that a visiting psychiatrist's confidential notes did not form part of Prison Department records. The confession was not a matter of public safety, since the prisoner was now deceased. It was therefore regarded as subject to professional confidence and the police were advised to contact the doctor directly.

Although it was not even certain that the two killings allegedly spoken about by the prisoner were the 'babes in the wood' murders, there were no other known cases in the relevant timeframe involving both a boy and girl as victims. And, since the inmate was now dead, there was now no way of establishing conclusively whether or not the confession was genuine, rather than another false confession such as those already encountered by the police in their investigations of the patients of Bristol mental hospitals. Mr Alan Hopkins, the then MP for Bristol, made his own enquiries of the Home Office and questions were asked in parliament, but the doctor remained steadfast – he would not reveal any more information and could not legally be forced to do so.

So officially, fifty years on, the tragic murders of Royston and June Sheasby remain unsolved and the case remains open to this day.

Bristol and County Asylum, 1906. (Author's collection)

BIBLIOGRAPHY & REFERENCES

BOOKS

Casswell, J.D. QC, *A Lance for Liberty*, London, George G. Harrap & Co. Ltd, 1961

Eddleston, John J., *The Encyclopaedia of Executions*, London, John Blake, 2004

Smith, Veronica, *Twenty Bristol Murders*, Bristol, Redcliffe Press Ltd, 1992

—*Murder and Mayhem in the West*, Bristol, Redcliffe Press Ltd, 1993

—*Foul Deeds and Suspicious Deaths in and around Bristol*, Barnsley, Wharncliffe Books, 2006

Wilson, Colin, (introduced by), *Murder in the Westcountry*, Bodmin, Bossiney Books, 1975

NEWSPAPERS

Bristol Evening Post
Bristol Mercury
Bristol Times and Mirror
News of the World
The Times

MAGAZINES

True Detective, July 1997

Certain websites have also been consulted in the compilation of this book, but since they have a habit of disappearing, to avoid frustration, they have not been cited.